The Rhetoric of Resistance to Prison Education

This book explores the discourse and rhetoric that resists and opposes postsecondary prison education. Positioning prison college programs as the best method to truly reduce recidivism, the book shows how the public – and by extension politicians – remain largely opposed to public funding for these programs, and how prisoners face internal resistance from their fellow inmates when pursuing higher education.

Utilizing methods including critical rhetorical history, media analysis, and autoethnography, the author explores and critiques the discourses which inhibit prison education. Cultural discourses, echoed through media portrayal of prisoners, produce criminals as both subhuman and always-already a threat to the public. This book highlights the history of rhetorical opposition to prison education; closely analyzes how convictism, prejudicial and discriminatory bias against prisoners, blocks education access and feeds the prison-industrial-complex an ever-recycled supply of free prison labor; and discusses the implications of prison education for understanding and contesting cultural discourses of criminality.

This book will be an important reference for scholars, graduate students, and upper-level undergraduates in the fields of Rhetoric, Criminal justice, and Sociology, as well as Media and Communication studies more generally, Politics, and Education studies.

Adam Key is Assistant Professor of Communication at the University of Arkansas at Monticello, USA. He spent most his early career teaching in Texas prisons. His research concerns the rhetorical, discursive, and mediated construction of deviance, particularly within the education system.

NCA Focus on Communication Studies
National Communication Association

The Twitter Presidency
Donald J. Trump and the Politics of White Rage
Brian L. Ott & Greg Dickinson

Mobile Devices and Technology in Higher Education
Jeffrey H. Kuznekoff, Stevie M. Munz and Scott Titsworth

The Rhetoric of Resistance to Prison Education
How the "War on Crime" Became the "War on Criminals"
Adam Key

The Rhetoric of Resistance to Prison Education

How the "War on Crime" Became the "War on Criminals"

Adam Key

Routledge
Taylor & Francis Group

NEW YORK AND LONDON

First published 2022
by Routledge
605 Third Avenue, New York, NY 10158

and by Routledge
2 Park Square, Milton Park, Abingdon, Oxon, OX14 4RN

Routledge is an imprint of the Taylor & Francis Group, an informa business

© 2022 Adam Key

The right of Adam Key to be identified as author of this work has been asserted in accordance with sections 77 and 78 of the Copyright, Designs and Patents Act 1988.

Library of Congress Cataloging-in-Publication Data
A catalog record for this title has been requested

ISBN: 978-1-032-03952-7 (hbk)
ISBN: 978-1-032-03959-6 (pbk)
ISBN: 978-1-003-18994-7 (ebk)

DOI: 10.4324/9781003189947

Typeset in Times New Roman
by codeMantra

For Matt May, who always believed in me and all his students. Solidarity Forever.

Contents

Tables

Acknowledgements

This book would not have been possible without my undergraduate research team of Natalie Craig, Alyssa Hooks, and Hannah Dumas as well as the Faculty Research Grant from the University of Arkansas at Monticello that supported it. I am also grateful for the enthusiastic support of Brontë Pearson, Erin Clement, Lexi Garcia, Mandy Morton, Jill Quarles, and Miles Ward whose kind words kept me going throughout this deeply involved project.

Preface

Years ago, when I gave my talk at TEDxTAMU, I started by telling the audience that the timing of the talk was excellent because I'd just gotten out of prison a few days prior. Indeed, I had but, as I assured the audience who was instantly uncomfortable when I made the initial statement, I was there because I taught classes for Lee College's Huntsville Center. Throughout the eight years I taught there, I was honored with the opportunity to teach over 1,000 men in six different units in and around Huntsville, TX. I started the first debate team in a Texas prison and hosted the only TEDx conference to ever take place behind Texan prison walls. Every year, I got to line up on stage at the chapel at the TDCJ Wynne Unit and watch dozens of my students walk across the stage to receive their diplomas. I was and am incredibly proud of them and grateful that I get to be part of their stories.

Despite my current career trajectory, I did not intend of becoming a prisoner rights advocate. Shortly after finishing my master's degree, I needed a job and the Huntsville Center was hiring. Even having spent years in the same city, I had no idea that college classes were being taught in prisons. My near decade there changed my life permanently. It got me a keynote address at an international research conference, took me to speak at Yale, on stage as a response speaker at TED Global 2017, to Kenya and Uganda to consult for prison college programs there, and earned me an invitation to speak at the United Nations Congress on Crime Prevention and Reduction.

Throughout all of these experiences, I still think about the TEDx audience's reaction. They went from looking panicked to laughing off my joke in a matter of moments, but what if I hadn't been joking? Would they have been receptive to my message if I was an ex-convict? Would a university like Texas A&M have even invited me to speak in the first place? They didn't know the men in my classrooms. They didn't laugh at their unceasing humor, applaud their progress, or see their struggles. They didn't see them as people at all, just always-already dangerous caricatures who they wanted to keep far far away from their neighborhoods. There was nothing especially bigoted about this audience. These were people who paid money to attend a TEDx conference on a Saturday afternoon at a high-ranking research institution. One could only assume they were more educated than most, but still they reacted in revulsion just the same at the thought that I could be a criminal.

The audience, and the public they represent, are the inspiration for this book. I wanted to understand how they, who'd likely never met a prisoner in their lives, could hate them so much that they'd oppose funding for programs like college classes in prison that actually reduce the crime rate. Utilizing a combination of original research and the utilization of parts of my dissertation, I constructed this text. Through a critical analysis of the rhetoric of politics and media, I believe I've found the answer and how to fight against it.

A Note on Language

There is a trend among scholars of prisoners and prison education led by the Underground Scholars Initiative in the University of California, Berkeley who published a style guide regarding use of specific terms by the media, the academy, and the public.[1] Their guide states to avoid using terms like "prisoner," "inmate," "convict," and "ex-convict." Instead, they propose the use of terms like "incarcerated person" and "system impacted." The justification for the guide "is about reclaiming our identity as people first," and the authors thank readers "for respecting us enough to treat us as humans."[2] I wholeheartedly disagree with this guide.

To avoid using language like "prisoner," "inmate," and "convict," implies that there is something inherently wrong with prisoners. Rather than being person first, this well-intentioned guide only furthers the social bias against prisoners. I take the opposite position. Instead of running from language and substituting it with bulky terminology not well understood by the public, my work here functions to help reclaim the terms "prisoner," "inmate," and "convict" in the same way that my LGBTQIA+ colleagues reclaimed the term "queer." You would not call me "a person who received a doctorate" because there is nothing immoral about having a PhD. In the same way, we use terms like "prisoner" because there is nothing immoral about being a prisoner.

Further, I take issue with the guide's stance that these terms make claims regarding guilt. I have a problem with this because it reflects the social bias, discussed more in Chapter 4, against prisoners who did, in fact, commit the crimes that resulted in their incarceration. Whether a person is actually guilty or innocent is immaterial to their worth as a person. By avoiding terms that might imply guilt, the guide once again furthers the same causes it claims to fight against.

As my formerly incarcerated student and colleague David Mains noted in a response to one of the authors on the Higher Ed in Prison listserv, the prison debate team at Lee College was proud to call themselves prisoners when they defeated Texas A&M University and Wiley College in the George Beto Invitational Debates. While I respect any individual's right to decide the terms by which others should refer to them, I refuse to accede to a small group making claims on behalf of large group, many of which who disagree with the guide's language. As such, I will use terms like "prisoner," "inmate," and "convict," within this book and encourage others to do the same.

"Language Guide for Communicating about Those Involved in the Carceral System." University of California at Berkeley, 2019.

Notes

1 "Language Guide for Communicating about Those Involved in the Carceral System," University of California at Berkeley, 2019.
2 Initiative, "Language Guide for Communicating about Those Involved in the Carceral System."

1   The Prison Classroom

2020. A year that will live in infamy. As historians record the tragic events of this tumultuous time, two specific occurrences are likely to dominate the discussion: the COVID-19 pandemic and the murder of George Floyd and the worldwide demonstrations that followed. As hundreds of thousands died in overcrowded ICUs and cities burned with the righteous indignation of protesters incensed by yet another person of color slain by those who had sworn to protect and serve, two other events emerged in response that were seemingly less remarkable when compared to the grand scale of international pandemics and protests. On March 29, as COVID began to surge and the United States went into lockdown, Texas Governor Greg Abbott issued Executive Order GA 13, prohibiting the release of any person currently in jail or prison with either a previous conviction or current arrest for a violent crime.[1] On June 3, eight days after Floyd's murder, conservative media personality Candace Owens tweeted a video where she claimed Floyd was neither a hero nor martyr because of his criminal record.[2]

These two seemingly unrelated events brought into sharp focus a largely taken-for-granted systemic bias within the United States that is the focus of this book: we hate people who break the law. Far from simply a stigma, this outright hatred, which I call convictism, is evident within the consequences of Abbott's executive order: he wanted them to die. Social distancing is physically impossible in prison. Inmates are housed two at a time in cells the size of a small walk-in closet, separated only by bars which would allow air and the virus to easily travel from person to person. While Texas regrettably remains a proponent of the death penalty, most prisoners are sentenced to a number of years, not to die. And die they did, as infections and deaths surged within Texas prisons after Abbott made their release impossible. Even after release, their criminal history becomes a permanent record that, in the eyes of people like Owens, means they cannot be

DOI: 10.4324/9781003189947-1

martyrs even when they are wrongfully executed by a corrupt system simply for the color of their skin.

Where does this near-universal hatred of prisoners and criminals originate? More importantly, why is it still tolerated? If you were to tell the average American that there is a group in this country that is not allowed to vote, not allowed to live in many places, and not allowed to work in certain jobs, you would no doubt see expressions of shock and disgust. However, as soon as you tell them you are speaking about former prisoners, their face will instantly transform from expressing surprise to contempt. You'll likely be met with some variation of "they deserve it" or "if you do the crime, you do the time." I remember candidly a conversation I had with my mother while I was teaching in prison. She loved to brag to her friends at church about the good works I was doing by helping inmates but had a markedly different response when they could come closer to home. During the conversation, she mentioned that a family friend who ran a pest control business was trying to hire new employees, so I suggested he hire some of my program's alumni that had been recently released. She responded matter-of-factly that he certainly couldn't hire them. After all, they had to go into people's homes. I remember staring at her blankly for a moment before saying something to the effect of "You really don't believe in what I do, do you?" For my mother and so many others, prisoners were great if they were a pet project for a volunteer or professional to try to reform, but they should be kept far away from her and other's houses.

The American public's tolerance of mistreatment regrettably does not end with forced exclusion from their communities after release. If you ask any middle schooler, they'll proudly tell you that Abraham Lincoln ended slavery with the Civil War. What they won't tell you, because their classes don't teach them, is that slavery is still alive and well within the United States. As Michelle Alexander's book *The New Jim Crow*[3] and Ava Duvernay's documentary *The 13th*[4] brilliantly illuminate, there is an exception to the 13th Amendment that still permits slavery as punishment for a crime. While some states pay inmates a few cents per hour, many like Texas where I used to teach pay them nothing. I spent eight years teaching over 1,000 enslaved men in the so-called land of the free.

It's also crucial to realize that this bias is not limited to one side of the political aisle. While conservatives have traditionally been in the "tough on crime" camp, liberals are often no better despite their claims to support prison abolition as well as prisoner and former prisoner rights. A prime example of this behavior is in the infamous case of the Stanford rapist, Brock Turner. After being found guilty of three felonies, Judge Aaron Persky sentenced him to six months, rather than the six years recommended by the prosecution, because a longer sentence would "have a severe impact on" Turner.[5] The national outrage was immediate. Both liberals and conservatives took to Twitter to express their anger at the lenient sentence. Persky was soon recalled by the voters of California, the first judge in the state to be removed since 1977.[6] Turner's sentencing became the impetus for revisions to the law which added a mandatory minimum sentence for sexual assault on an unconscious person. The law's passage was largely driven by progressives in one of the country's bluest states, a group that ostensibly supports the elimination of mandatory minimum sentences.[7] Under the right circumstances, even groups committed to abolishing prisons will push for harsher sentences.

This is not to say, of course, that Turner's actions were not horrific and that he was undeserving of punishment. He certainly did. Despite his recall, however, the fact remains that what Persky said was correct. A long prison sentence would undoubtedly have a "severe impact" on Turner or anyone else. Instead of calling for prison reform that would mean prison sentences would have a less severe impact, the public decided they were perfectly fine with prison being a barbaric and torturous place so long as Turner spent significant time there.

It is also true that some, but not all, of the public's outrage stemmed from Turner being one more affluent white man whose privilege shielded him from consequences. Those reasons, however, are tangential to their anger. While the history of the American prison system shows that BIPOC and members of lower economic classes have been unfairly arrested, prosecuted, and sentenced compared to their majority counterparts, the public would have been nearly just as furious had a Black man living below the poverty line had received six months for attempted rape. Furthermore, numerous other works, like those from Michelle Alexander and Bruce Western, address the intersections of incarceration, race, and poverty. Instead of trying to replicate their work, this book seeks to examine a different but related systemic bias.

This is a country that decries rape culture, but still makes jokes about prominent figures "dropping the soap" when they are sentenced to prison. It is a place where professors will argue against the disenfranchisement of felons while they work for universities that ask for applicant's criminal history along with their admissions materials. It is a nation where 2nd Amendment activists will argue for their God-given right to own military grade assault weapons but think that God made an exception for the formerly incarcerated who want to buy a firearm.

At first glance, it might be easy to assume that people hate criminals because of the crimes they commit. That is, that the public hates crime and therefore criminals for perpetrating them. That would seem to align with the notions of the "War on Crime" and being "tough on crime." On critical reflection, however, it is apparent that citizens of the United States hate criminals far more than they hate crime itself. The primary evidence of this is that the public remains stalwartly opposed to programs that actually reduce the crime rate because they benefit prisoners, namely postsecondary prison education: It wasn't always this way, however. In this book, I explore the rhetoric, both political and mediated, which got us to the place where we as a country would rather see prisoners die of a deadly disease than the crime rate fall. Through a critical rhetorical history of the past and the present, I argue that public resistance to postsecondary prison education is the result of convictism, a systemic bias against criminals and prisoners that has developed the "War on Crime" into the "War on Criminals."

Nothing Works... Or Does It?

The infamous Martinson Report came to the conclusion that "nothing works" in the rehabilitation of criminals.[8] More recent research has demonstrated the opposite conclusion.[9] The collective body of knowledge regarding rehabilitation within carceral environments shows that education works as a powerful force "to reduce recidivism by enhancing employability, increasing self-esteem and fostering personal growth."[10] More recently, a study by the RAND Corporation demonstrating a concrete relationship between postsecondary prison education and recidivism led the Obama administration to implement the Second Chance Pell Grant Program, partially restoring federal financial aid to prison college students.[11] Clearly, despite the Martinson Report's claim, something is working.[12]

In general, the recidivism rate in the United States is extremely high. According to the most recent report released by the Bureau of Justice Statistics, five of every six people released from state prisons will be arrested within nine years.[13] More specifically, 68% are arrested within the first three years, 79% by the six-year mark, and by nine years 83% have been arrested at least once. The report also found that those previously incarcerated for property and drug crimes were more likely to recidivate than those convicted of violent offenses. Education, however, demonstrated a significant effect in bringing these numbers down. The RAND study found an average reduction of 48% in the recidivism rate of those people who took part in any type of post-secondary education program while in prison.[14] Other research have shown that the recidivism rate for those who complete an Associate's degree is 14%, down to 5.6% for those leaving with a Bachelor's degree, and at 0% for those who earn a master's degree behind bars.[15] These numbers are, of course, averages. Some programs fare far better in reducing recidivism than this. Lee College's Huntsville Center, where I was previously employed, has reported a reduction down to a 5% recidivism rate for those who completed their Associate's degree program.[16]

Why does education have such a dramatic effect on reducing the crime rate of those released from prison? To find the answer, one must start with the type of crimes they are committing. According to data compiled by the Prison Policy Institute, only 37.4% of the 1.6 million men[17] and women currently incarcerated in federal, state, and local jails and prisons are serving time for violent crimes,[18] meaning that nearly two-thirds of men and women in prison are behind bars for property or drug crimes.[19] This, however, only captures the image of those incarcerated. When looking into arrests overall, the number is even more telling. According to the most recent data available from the FBI, there are 935,000 violent crimes committed annually compared to 6.9 million property crimes and an additional 1.5 million arrests for drug offenses, the majority of which were for possession.[20] All told, the data shows nearly two of every three people in prison and nearly nine of ten people who commit crimes do so for economic or drug-related reasons.

What does the majority of crimes being economic and drug related tell us about why education reduces the recidivism rate? We know already that prisoners tend to have a significantly lower education level than the general population. For example, two of every three prisoners are incarcerated with at most a high school diploma or GED, compared to one of every two non-incarcerated Americans.[21] In fact, 40% of prisoners dropped out, failed out, or were kicked out of the K-12 education system prior to being locked up.[22] In total, upon incarceration, two of every five prisoners do not have a high school diploma or GED. Of the remaining three of every five prisoners that have a diploma or more, a third only has that. With the majority entering already educationally disadvantaged, the prison system offers them little opportunity to advance their learning. Only four out of ten prisoners complete any kind of formal education within prison and the overwhelming majority of those receive a GED.[23] Only 7% earn a certificate of any type from a college or trade school, while only 2% leave prison with an Associate's degree. This is not due to a lack of interest, but a lack of availability. Research by the US Department of Education shows that seven of ten prisoners want to enroll in some sort of academic program, with 40% of those wanting to earn some level of college degree.[24]

With a lack of education before and after prison, the formerly incarcerated find themselves in an undesirable economic predicament upon release. In the present labor market, they do far worse than the average American without a prison record. According to an analysis of data from the Internal Revenue Service, only half of people released from prison are able to find formal employment of any sort within the first year of their release.[25] For those that find jobs at all, they work fewer weeks and earn lower wages than comparable workers who have not been to prison.[26] The median annual earnings in the first year of release are only $1,000, less than someone with a full-time minimum wage job and about $2,700 below the poverty line for an individual.[27] This economic hardship, both historically and currently, contributes to crime and recidivism rates.

The Relationship between Crime and Class[28]

As Bruce Western[29] noted, one of main causes of the prison boom was the collapse of inner-city industrial centers in the 1970s.[30] In the beginnings of globalization and the post-industrial age, communities began to collapse as unskilled factory jobs requiring little formal education began to rapidly disappear. As factories in city centers began to close and jobs members of working-class communities moved en masse to countries with cheaper labor, companies began to focus on hiring only highly skilled workers with formal education. The now unemployed workers, having no means to access legal employment, began turning to the underground economies of illegal narcotics sales.

In response to the rising drug economy, President Richard Nixon launched an initiative to crack down on both narcotics users and dealers known as the "War on Drugs." The lasting effects of the "War on Drugs" and the companion "War on Crime" are still felt today. While crime rates among the poor, especially violent crimes, spiked in the 1980s, they had diminished by the year 2000 but incarceration rates continue to rise. "Although disadvantaged men became more law-abiding, their chances of going to prison rose to historic levels."[31] Western's analysis of the data revealed three primary causes for the increased imprisonment of the poor: first, "a significant increase in the use of imprisonment for those who are convicted of a crime;" second, "those who go to prison are now serving longer sentences;" and finally, "a dramatic increase in the prosecution and incarceration of drug offenders."[32]

In as much as economic inequality is a cause of incarceration, it is also an effect. Western argued that incarceration is a "key life event that triggers a cumulative spiral of disadvantage. Incarceration reduces not just the level of wages, it also slows wage growth over the life course and restricts the kinds of jobs former inmates might find."[33] The three reasons offered by Western for the effects of this spiral are the stigma of incarceration, a reduction in human capital, and a lack of social capital.

Stigma, according to Erving Goffman, is the means by which society enacts and justifies the exclusion of certain individuals from acceptance.[34] Goffman specified three distinct types of stigma: character, group identity, and physicality. Stigmas of character include perceptions of attributes including "weak will, domineering or unnatural passions... [and] dishonesty."[35] Group identity stigmas tend to be treated as "tribal" and result from a person's association with an undesirable group.[36] Finally, stigmas of physicality come from "abominations of the body... [and] various physical deformities."[37] While the bodies of former prisoners may or may not be marked by tattoos indicating their time as inmates, the primary means of stigma experienced are character and group identity.

The stigma attached to former prisoners seeking employment occurs through both legal and social means. In terms of law, they might be precluded by statute from entering certain professions or earning licenses to practice particular careers. For instance, in many jurisdictions, a former prisoner cannot have a profession that involves entering client's homes or earn a license to practice law. Related to this, in almost every state, employers are legally able to deny an applicant a job on the basis of criminal conviction.[38] Further, a significant number of colleges and universities (including Texas A&M where I earned my doctorate) ask about criminal convictions in applications for enrollment, cutting former prisoners off from access from higher education degrees necessary for many professions. Even absent laws, however, many employers view a conviction as a marker that the applicant is untrustworthy and pass them over for hiring. In either case, legal or social, former prisoners bear the marks of stigmas that view their character and association as suspect.

In addition to suffering from negative stigmas, many released prisoners also have deficiencies in human capital, their ability to be productive workers, as a result of their years incarcerated. Western stated that time in prison "may undermine job skills by removing men from the marketplace from which they might otherwise gain work experience."[39] With rare exceptions, like the mattress factories in Texas prisons, very few prisoner work assignments provide skills that are translatable to work in the outside world. A long-term assignment as a janitor or a kitchen worker does little to qualify a former inmate for jobs beyond low-paying entry level positions. Even if they are able to find work in these types of positions, their lack of presence in the legal workforce means that, in adulthood, they will start at base wages having missed opportunities for raises and promotions due to incarceration. Furthermore, behaviors necessary "for survival in prison – suspicion of strangers, aggressiveness, withdrawal from social interaction – are inconsistent with work routines outside."[40] The cumulative effect of all of these factors is a severe reduction in human capital as a result of time spent behind bars.

Former prisoners additionally suffer from a lack of social capital. Being removed from their home communities for a significant period of time tends to deaccess them from their previous social networks. In their place, former prisoners' networks consist primarily of other inmates, which statutes may prevent them from legally contacting while one or both is still on parole. This becomes a problem in the job search as "workers regularly find jobs through social contacts who can then vouch for job applicants to employers, [therefore] job seekers without social ties to legitimate employment opportunities face significant disadvantages in the labor market."[41] Without a strong social network to guide them to legal employment, many former prisons return to the underground economies that landed them behind bars in the first place.

In an attempt to summarize their predicament, Western reiterated the claims of life course theories of deviance in relation to boys and men in low economic classes, writing that "the home life and neighborhoods of the middle class erect barriers to criminal behavior. A stable marriage, like a steady job, creates everyday routines for husbands who might otherwise be on the streets, getting into trouble."[42] When lower classes lack these things, their imprecise routines allow for more time to engage in lawbreaking. This is not to say, however, that no jobs were or are available to lower class boys and men. In an ethnographic study of youth in Spanish Harlem, Phillipe Bourgois found that "the insult of working for entry-level wages amidst extraordinary opulence is painful"[43] for his subjects. As such, many opt to engage in criminal behavior resulting in their incarceration.

Prison Education Reduces Crime by Providing Capital

Earning a college degree behind bars provides considerable solutions for the capital deficits Western identified. First and foremost, it provides the human capital most prisoners are deprived of during their sentences. In particular, CTE programs, which remain the primary form of postsecondary prison education, train inmates in valuable trades which result not only in them being hired but paid substantial wages. For example, students who majored in welding at my former employer often immediately left prison and walked into positions paying upwards of $25 an hour. They are not alone in this result.

Analysis by RAND found that participation in education programs of any type increased the odds of finding employment for former prisoners by 12% and any type of vocational training raised it to a 22% overall increase.[44] Furthermore, a joint analysis by Georgetown University and the Vera Institute of Justice found that adding postsecondary education would increase the odds of employment by an additional 5%.[45] While no national level study has been conducted on individual wages for graduates of prison college programs, state-level studies have found increased wages for former prisoners with degrees in Minnesota[46] and those receiving any form of education in Florida.[47] Furthermore, the Vera/Georgetown study was able to estimate that an increase in prison education participation could produce anywhere from 45 to 68 million dollars in increased earnings yearly.[48] Additionally, the low recidivism rates of inmates who earn degrees behind bars would collectively save states up to $548 million per year, not including the savings gained in the federal prison system.

In regard to social capital, college programs behind bars provide this as well. In addition to the degree earned, one of the primary benefits for any college graduate is their alumni organization and its ability to procure jobs. For example, as a graduate of Texas A&M University, I am well-versed in the power of the Aggie network in finding jobs. Graduates from prison college programs receive the same degrees and diplomas as their non-incarcerated counterparts and would thus have access to the same alumni networks. The one remaining factor Western identified is stigma. As a critical examination of the history of prison education programs shows, the level of stigma based upon incarceration significantly fluctuated throughout American history.

History of Prison Education, 1791–1994

While American prison education may seem like a recent phenomenon, the concept of educating prisoners is, in fact, nearly as old as American prisons themselves. Fifteen years after the founding of the United States, the Quakers created the nation's first formal prison in 1791.[49] In addition to the promotion of public safety, their main concern was the rehabilitation and reincorporation of prisoners into society. To that end, they created a school inside the prison in 1798. While this primarily consisted of mandatory religious education, a type that would not pass muster under modern understandings of separation of church and state, the Quakers were emphatic that providing an education was a crucial part of the prison experience.

This emphasis would persist until the late 19th century following the Industrial Revolution. At that point, the public view of prisoners shifted from errants in need of education to a source of cheap labor.[50] New York, for instance, pioneered the use of prisoners in industrial mass production. Gone were the days where prisoners would attend classes to better themselves and instead replaced with long shifts mindlessly producing goods and performing other tasks that laid the groundwork for what is now known as the prison-industrial complex.

While the pendulum had swung wildly between viewing prisoners as students in need of education and cogs on the industrial machine, it briefly landed in the center at the beginning of the 20th century. At that time, a balance was struck between the goals of teaching inmates skills that would help them be successful on release and meeting the prison's desires to have skilled inmate labor.[51] The first postsecondary prison education programs, then, would be vocational and technical education, which still persist today as the dominant form of education available to prisoners.[52] Incarcerated students would learn trades which would enable them both to perform work in and for the prisons as well as increasing their opportunities for gainful employment upon release. This balance was, however, regrettably short-lived as the Great Depression eliminated the public's desire for these programs and the pendulum would once again shift toward forced labor.

The pendulum would remain in place until it would once again wildly swing in the other direction in the mid-20th century. The enabling force behind this shift was the passage of Title IV of the

Higher Education Act in 1965, creating a federal program to provide financial assistance to low-income college students in a program that would eventually be called Pell Grants. For good reason, Silva calls this law's passage the "single most important event in the development of higher education for prisoners."[53] At the time of its implementation, prisoners were not excluded from the program. However, eligibility was not enough on its own. To receive a higher education, inmates would need classes to be offered behind bars. They would find an ally in what now seems like the most unlikely of places: the state of Texas.

Modernly, Texas has a well-deserved reputation for abusing prisoners. When I was in Uganda consulting for the African Prisons Project – since rebranded as Justice Changemakers – I had the opportunity to speak to a support group for prisoners with HIV. When I told the group I taught classes in American prisons, they were intrigued and asked me where I taught. When I told them Texas, there was an awkward silence amongst the previously chatty group. They exchanged knowing looks among each other before their leader broke the tense moment, telling me "Tell your students we pray for them." In a maximum-security unit in a country known for child soldiers and the HIV epidemic, they pitied prisoners in Texas. That Texas has an education program in its prisons at all, much less one of the oldest and most established in the nation, is primarily the result of the work of one man: Dr George Beto.[54]

A former Lutheran minister, Beto served on the Texas Prison Board from 1953 to 1959 where he was responsible for the creation of the first General Education Program for prisoners in American history in 1956. He left the board in 1959 to become the president of Concordia Theological Seminary until 1962. During that time, he toured prisons across many European nations and served on various advisory bodies. Beto would return to Texas prison administration as the director of the then-Texas Department of Corrections. Observing that the majority of prisoners consisted of "the poor, the stupid, and the inept," Beto implemented a number of educational programs to help promote rehabilitation.[55] These included the creation of the Windham Independent School District, a first of its kind prison secondary education program, in 1969. Following that, he issued an invitation of colleges to teach classes inside prison walls. One of the original higher education institutions was Lee College, my former employer, who established the Huntsville Center in Huntsville, TX in 1965.

The Huntsville Center is one of the nation's oldest and longest standing postsecondary prison education programs.[56] While it is not the original – it was preceded by Southern Illinois University at Carbondale who began a now defunct prison college program in 1953 – it was one of the first to be constituted under Title IV.[57] The original faculty were employees who voluntarily committed themselves to educating prisoners, despite numerous hurdles. For the first 13 years of the program, Lee College did not have an office in Huntsville. Instead, faculty maintained offices and their residences in Baytown, TX outside Houston where Lee's main campus is located. According to Gos, "Throughout those years, academic faculty members made the 190-mile round trip to the center twice a week to teach classes face-to-face."[58]

According to Jerry Alston, then Dean of Instruction at the Huntsville Center, "The Lee College-TDC association aims to return men to society in a condition to assume positions of freedom in the general community."[59] While the program, like most involved in postsecondary prison education, has historically offered technical education classes where students learn professions ranging from horticulture to computer networking, the Huntsville Center has always placed an emphasis on academic classes.

> Technical-vocational courses made their first appearance during the spring semester of 1966. But the initial emphasis on academic courses in the humanities and social sciences continues in all programs based upon the rationale that such courses give prisoners a new insight into whom they are and what they may become. The assumption underlying this emphasis is that prisoners who are later confronted with ethical, social and/or political issues will be better equipped to tolerate alternative views, issues and politics.[60]

Lee was not alone in adopting a dual emphasis on vocational and academic skill-building within prison classrooms. While the focus primarily remained on technical and vocational classes, the introduction of academic classes became a more popular trend as years passed. Lee was a pioneer in the field of prison education, but it didn't remain lonely for long. By 1973, 182 colleges and universities were teaching classes behind bars. That number bloomed to 267 by 1976 and peaked at 350 in 1982.[61] While community colleges provided the lion's share of classes, prisoners at various units across the country could earn Bachelor's and even Master's degrees.[62] For nearly three decades, higher education became a fixture within the American prison system. It seemed that the pendulum had finally settled in place until it swung wildly once again in 1994.

Notes

1 Greg Abbott, Executive order GA-13 relating to detention in county and municipaljails during the COVID-19 disaster, (2020).
2 Candace Owens, "Confession: #GeorgeFloyd is neither a martyr or a hero. But I hope his family gets justice," (Twitter, 3:37pm June 3 2020), https://twitter.com/RealCandaceO/status/1268280610818101248.
3 Michelle Alexander, *The new Jim Crow: Mass incarceration in the age of colorblindness* (New York: The New Press, 2012).
4 Ava Duvernay, "The 13th," (Netflix: Forward Movement/Kandoo Films, 2016).
5 Aaron Persky, "Stanford sexual assault: Read the full text of the judge's controversial decision," *The Guardian* 2016, https://www.theguardian.com/us-news/2016/jun/14/stanford-sexual-assault-read-sentence-judge-aaron-persky.
6 Maggie Astor, "California voters remove judge Aaron Persky, who gave a 6-monthsentenceforsexualassault," *TheNew YorkTimes*2018,https://www.nytimes.com/2018/06/06/us/politics/judge-persky-brock-turner-recall.html#:~:text=Aaron%20Persky%2C%20the%20California%20judge%20who%20drew%20national,recalled%20in%20California%20in%20more%20than%2080%20years.
7 Matt Ford, "How Brock Turner changed california's rape laws," *The Atlantic* 2016, https://www.theatlantic.com/news/archive/2016/10/california-law-brock-turner/502562/.
8 Robert Martinson, "What works?-Questions and answers about prison reform," *The Public Interest* 35, (1974): 22–54.
9 David B Wilson, Catherine A Gallagher, and Doris L MacKenzie, "A meta-analysis of corrections-based education, vocation, and work programs for adult offenders," *Journal of Research in Crime and Delinquency* 37, no. 4 (2000): 347–68.
10 Mary Ellen Batiuk et al., "Disentangling the effects of correctional education are current policies misguided? An event history analysis," *Criminal Justice* 5, no. 1 (2005): 56.
11 Lois M Davis et al., *Evaluating the effectiveness of correctional education: A meta-analysis of programs that provide education to incarcerated adults* (Santa Monica, CA: Rand Corporation, 2013).
12 Martinson, "What works?-Questions and answers about prison reform."
13 Matthew R Durose, Alexia D Cooper, and Howard N Snyder, *Recidivism of prisoners released in 30 states in 2005: Patterns from 2005 to 2010*, vol. 28 (US Department of Justice, Office of Justice Programs, Bureau of Justice Statistics, 2014).
14 Davis et al., *Evaluating the effectiveness of correctional education.*
15 James Beard, Marcia Johnson, and JaPaula Kemp, Proposal to reduce recidivism rates in Texas, 2003, Thurgood Marshall School of Law, http://www.tsulaw.edu/centers/ECI/pubs_files/Criminal%20Justice/Recidivism%20Position%20Paper%20-%20PDF%5BFinal%5D.pdf.
16 Jerry G Alston, "The role of the community college in instruction for the incarcerated," *Community College Review* 9, no. 2 (1981): 10–14.
17 This does not include people being held over for trial but who have not been convicted.

18 I differ from the Uniform Crime Report in that I classify robbery as a property/economic crime, rather than a violent one. While it does involve some type of violence or threat of violence, much like its companion crime burglary, the goal of commission is economic.

19 Wendy Sawyer and Peter Wagner, "Mass incarceration: The whole pie 2020," news release, 2020, https://www.prisonpolicy.org/reports/pie2020.html.

20 Federal Bureau of Investigation, Crime in the United States, (Department of Justice, 2019).

21 Bobby D Rampey et al., Highlights from the U.S. PIAAC survey of incarcerated adults: Their skills, work experience, education, and training, NCES 2016-40 (2016).

22 Caroline Wolf Harlow, Education and correctional populations, NCJ 195670 (2003).

23 Rampey et al., Highlights from the U.S. PIAAC survey of incarcerated adults.

24 Rampey et al., Highlights from the U.S. PIAAC survey of incarcerated adults.

25 Adam Looney and Nicholas Turner, *Work and opportunity before and after incarceration* (Washington, DC: The Brookings Institution, 2018).

26 Steven Raphael, "The employment prospects of ex-offenders," *Focus* 25, no. 2 (2007): 21–6.

27 Looney and Turner, *Work and opportunity before and after incarceration.*

28 This section is adapted from Adam Key, "In the first degree: A study of effective discourse in postsecondary prison education" (PhD. Dissertation, Texas A&M University, 2018).

29 Western's book is perhaps the definitive history of the relationship of crime and class in the United States. Rather than attempt to reinvent the wheel, I largely summarize his findings within this subsection.

30 Bruce Western, *Punishment and inequality in America* (New York: Russell Sage Foundation, 2006).

31 Western, *Punishment and inequality in America*, 50.

32 Western, *Punishment and inequality in America*, 50.

33 Western, *Punishment and inequality in America*, 109.

34 Erving Goffman, *Stigma: Notes on the management of spoiled identity* (New York: Simon and Schuster, 1963).

35 Goffman, *Stigma*, 4.

36 Goffman, *Stigma*, 4.

37 Goffman, *Stigma*, 4.

38 Western, *Punishment and inequality in America.*

39 Western, *Punishment and inequality in America*, 113.

40 Western, *Punishment and inequality in America*, 113.

41 Western, *Punishment and inequality in America*, 114.

42 Western, *Punishment and inequality in America*, 36.

43 Philippe Bourgois, "Crack in Spanish Harlem: Culture and economy in the inner city," *Anthropology Today* 5, no. 4 (1989): 8.

44 Durose, Cooper, and Snyder, *Recidivism of prisoners released in 30 states in 2005*, 28.

45 Patrick Oakford et al., *Investing in futures: Economic and fiscal benefits of postsecondary education in prison* (Vera Institute of Justice, 2019), https://www.vera.org/downloads/publications/investing-in-futures.pdf.

46 Grant Duwe and Valerie Clark, "The effects of prison-based educational programming on recidivism and employment," *The Prison Journal* 94, no. 4 (2014): 454–78.

47 Rosa Minhyo Cho and John H Tyler, "Does prison-based adult basic education improve postrelease outcomes for male prisoners in Florida?" *Crime & Delinquency* 59, no. 7 (2013): 975–1005.

48 Oakford et al., *Investing in futures: Economic and fiscal benefits of postsecondary education in prison.*

49 LeRoy B DePuy, "The Walnut Street prison: Pennsylvania's first penitentiary," *Pennsylvania History: A Journal of Mid-Atlantic Studies* 18, no. 2 (1951): 130–44.

50 Howard B Gill, "Correctional philosophy and architecture," *The Journal of Criminal Law, Criminology, and Police Science* 53, no. 3 (1962): 312–22.

51 Shakoor A Ward, "Career and technical education in United States prisons: What have we learned?" *Journal of Correctional Education* 60, no. 3 (2009):191–200.

52 Ward, "Career and technical education in United States prisons: What have we learned?"

53 W Silva, "A brief history of prison higher education in the United States," in *Higher education in prison: A contradiction in terms?*, ed. M Williford (Phoenix, AZ: Oryx Press, 1994), 26.

54 Paul M Lucko, "Beto, George John," in *Handbook of Texas online* (Texas State Historical Association, n.d.), https://www.tshaonline.org/handbook/entries/beto-george-john.

55 Lucko, "Beto, George John."

56 Alston, "The role of the community college in instruction for the incarcerated."

57 Susanna Spaulding, "Borderland stories about teaching college in prison," *New Directions for Community Colleges* 20, no. 15 (2011): 73–83.

58 Michael Gos, "Nontraditional student access to OWI," in *Foundational principles of online writing instruction*, ed. B Hewett and K DePew (Anderson, SC: Parlor Press, 2015), 337.

59 Alston, "The role of the community college in instruction for the incarcerated," 12.

60 Alston, "The role of the community college in instruction for the incarcerated," 113.

61 Christopher Zoukis, *College for convicts: The case for higher education in American prisons* (Jefferson, SC: McFarland, 2014).

62 Zoukis, *College for convicts.*

References

Abbott, Greg. *Executive Order Ga-13 Relating to Detention in County and Municipal jails during the Covid-19 Disaster*, 2020.

Alexander, Michelle. *The New Jim Crow: Mass Incarceration in the Age of Colorblindness.* New York: The New Press, 2012.

Alston, Jerry G. "The Role of the Community College in Instruction for the Incarcerated." *Community College Review* 9, no. 2 (1981): 10–14.

Astor, Maggie. "California Voters Remove Judge Aaron Persky, Who Gave a 6-Month Sentence for Sexual Assault." *The New York Times*, 2018. https://www.nytimes.com/2018/06/06/us/politics/judge-persky-brock-turner-recall.html#:~:text=Aaron%20Persky%2C%20the%20California%20judge%20who%20drew%20national, recalled%20in%20California%20in%20more%20than%2080%20years.

Batiuk, Mary Ellen, Karen F Lahm, Matthew McKeever, Norma Wilcox, and Pamela Wilcox. "Disentangling the Effects of Correctional Education Are Current Policies Misguided? An Event History Analysis." *Criminal Justice* 5, no. 1 (2005): 55–74.

Beard, James, Marcia Johnson, and JaPaula Kemp. Proposal to Reduce Recidivism Rates in Texas. http://www.tsulaw.edu/centers/ECI/pubs_files/Criminal%20Justice/Recidivism%20Position%20Paper%20-%20PDF%5B-Final%5D.pdf.

Bourgois, Philippe. "Crack in Spanish Harlem: Culture and Economy in the Inner City." *Anthropology Today* 5, no. 4 (1989): 6–11.

Cho, Rosa Minhyo, and John H Tyler. "Does Prison-Based Adult Basic Education Improve Postrelease Outcomes for Male Prisoners in Florida?" *Crime & Delinquency* 59, no. 7 (2013): 975–1005.

Davis, Lois M, Robert Bozick, Jennifer L Steele, Jessica Saunders, and Jeremy NV Miles. *Evaluating the Effectiveness of Correctional Education: A Meta-Analysis of Programs That Provide Education to Incarcerated Adults.* Santa Monica, CA: Rand Corporation, 2013.

DePuy, LeRoy B. "The Walnut Street Prison: Pennsylvania's First Penitentiary." *Pennsylvania History: A Journal of Mid-Atlantic Studies* 18, no. 2 (1951): 130–44.

Durose, Matthew R, Alexia D Cooper, and Howard N Snyder. *Recidivism of Prisoners Released in 30 States in 2005: Patterns from 2005 to 2010.* Vol. 28: US Department of Justice, Office of Justice Programs, Bureau of Justice Statistics, 2014.

Duvernay, Ava. "The 13th." Netflix: Forward Movement/Kandoo Films, 2016.

Duwe, Grant, and Valerie Clark. "The Effects of Prison-Based Educational Programming on Recidivism and Employment." *The Prison Journal* 94, no. 4 (2014): 454–78.

Ford, Matt. "How Brock Turner Changed California's Rape Laws." *The Atlantic*, 2016. https://www.theatlantic.com/news/archive/2016/10/california-law-brock-turner/502562/.

Gill, Howard B. "Correctional Philosophy and Architecture." *The Journal of Criminal Law, Criminology, and Police Science* 53, no. 3 (1962): 312–22.

Goffman, Erving. *Stigma: Notes on the Management of Spoiled Identity.* New York: Simon and Schuster, 1963.

Gos, Michael. "Nontraditional Student Access to Owi." In *Foundational Principles of Online Writing Instruction*, edited by B Hewett and K DePew. Anderson, SC: Parlor Press, 2015: 309–46.

Harlow, Caroline Wolf. *Education and Correctional Populations*, 2003: 1–12.

Investigation, Federal Bureau of. *Crime in the United States*: Department of Justice, 2019.

Key, Adam. "In the First Degree: A Study of Effective Discourse in Post-secondary Prison Education." Ph.D. Dissertation, Texas A&M University, 2018.

Looney, Adam, and Nicholas Turner. *Work and Opportunity before and after Incarceration*. Washington, DC: The Brookings Institute, 2018: 1–20.

Lucko, Paul M. "Beto, George John." In *Handbook of Texas Online*. Texas State Historical Association, n.d. https://www.tshaonline.org/handbook/entries/beto-george-john.

Martinson, Robert. "What Works?-Questions and Answers about Prison Reform." *The Public Interest* 35, (1974): 22–54.

Oakford, Patrick, Cara Brumfield, Casey Goldvale, Margaret diZerega, and Fred Patrick. *Investing in Futures: Economic and Fiscal Benefits of Postsecondary Education in Prison*. https://www.vera.org/downloads/publications/investing-in-futures.pdf.

Owens, Candace. "Confession: #Georgefloyd Is Neither a Martyr or a Hero. But I Hope His Family Gets Justice." Twitter, 3:37pm June 3 2020. https://twitter.com/RealCandaceO/status/1268280610818101248.

Persky, Aaron. "Stanford Sexual Assault: Read the Full Text of the Judge's Controversial Decision." *The Guardian*, 2016. https://www.theguardian.com/us-news/2016/jun/14/stanford-sexual-assault-read-sentence-judge-aaron-persky.

Rampey, Bobby D, Shelly Keiper, Leyla Mohadjer, Tom Krenzke, Jianzhu Li, Nina Thornton, Jaquie Hogan, Holly Xie, and Stephen Provasnik. *Highlights from the U.S. Piaac Survey of Incarcerated Adults: Their Skills, Work Experience, Education, and Training*, 2016.

Raphael, Steven. "The Employment Prospects of Ex-Offenders." *Focus* 25, no. 2 (2007): 21–26.

Sawyer, Wendy, and Peter Wagner. "Mass Incarceration: The Whole Pie 2020." news release, 2020. https://www.prisonpolicy.org/reports/pie2020.html.

Silva, W. "A Brief History of Prison Higher Education in the United States." In *Higher Education in Prison: A Contradiction in Terms?*, edited by M Williford. Phoenix, AZ: Oryx Press, 1994: 17–31.

Spaulding, Susanna. "Borderland Stories about Teaching College in Prison." *New Directions for Community Colleges* 20, no. 15 (2011): 73–83.

Ward, Shakoor A. "Career and Technical Education in United States Prisons: What Have We Learned?". *Journal of Correctional Education* 60, no. 3 (2009): 191–200.

Western, Bruce. *Punishment and Inequality in America*. New York: Russell Sage Foundation, 2006.

Wilson, David B, Catherine A Gallagher, and Doris L MacKenzie. "A Meta-Analysis of Corrections-Based Education, Vocation, and Work Programs for Adult Offenders." *Journal of Research in Crime and Delinquency* 37, no. 4 (2000): 347–68.

Zoukis, Christopher. *College for Convicts: The Case for Higher Education in American Prisons.* Jefferson, SC: McFarland, 2014.

2 Kids before Cons?

"Won't somebody please think of the children?"[1] This exclamation by *The Simpsons* character Helen Lovejoy is most often used as a humorous quip. Unfortunately, however, it accurately summarizes much of the modern position in opposition to postsecondary prison education. From the elimination of funding for prison education in the 1990sto opposition campaigns to public funding of prison college programs in the last decade, opponents repeatedly framed the issue as one that pits prisoners against innocent law-abiding children. As this chapter will demonstrate, much like Lovejoy herself, this position is wholly out of touch with reality.

At the end of the previous chapter, I provided a history of the first two centuries of American prison education. During that time period, the pendulum of public opinion repeatedly swung between two opposite poles: prisoners as savages whose only purpose is providing cheap labor and prisoners as people whose potential can be reached through education. In the 1960s, the pendulum seemed to finally fix in place at the latter pole, only to abruptly swing to the opposite side in the 1990s when federal funding for incarcerated college students was completely eliminated. While the policy change was overnight, the events that preceded it grew steadily during the three-decade Renaissance of the prison classroom.

The Empire Strikes Back

Taking the long view of American politics, a similar pendulum swinging pattern emerges that almost mirrors the plot of the *Star Wars* franchise. Each time the liberal Rebellion moves the nation progressively forward, the conservative Empire strikes back. At the end of the Civil War, the country passed the 13th, 14th, and 15th Amendments and instituted Reconstruction. Two years later, an 1877 compromise made to ensure the certification of the election of Rutherford B. Hayes led

DOI: 10.4324/9781003189947-2

to Union troops being withdrawn from previous Confederate states.[2] Now unfettered by military supervision, the conservative South struck back and implemented a plethora of racist polices known as Jim Crow laws and exploited a provision of the 13th Amendment to re-enslave Black Americans through incarceration.[3] A century later, the nation's liberals pushed the country forward again. The Civil Rights Acts of 1964 and 1968 were passed, *Roe v. Wade* ensured the right to reproductive freedom would be protected, divorce became legalized nationally giving women the opportunity to leave abusive marriages, and the late Ruth Bader Ginsburg successfully chipped away at sex discrimination laws through a series of Supreme Court victories. In response, conservatives struck back again as Richard Nixon began the "War on Drugs" as a furtherance of Lyndon B. Johnson's "War on Crime;" Jerry Falwell started the Moral Majority; and the country elected former television and movie star Ronald Reagan who would deregulate industry and favor big business over the American public under the failed notion of "trickle-down economics."

Finally, America moved forward in 2008 with the election of Barack Obama, its first Black president, whose era saw the passage of a law to provide health insurance to the public, the expansion of Title IX protections of gender equality and against sexual assault in the nation's colleges and universities, and the Supreme Court's legalization of same-sex marriage. Eight years later, the right-wing empire would make its most decisive strike to date, electing a second television star to the highest office in the land: Donald Trump. The follies and regressive polices of the Trump administration could and should be the subject of entire books. These included an attempted Muslim ban, a family separation policy that turned detention facilities into concentration camps, gutting Title IX protections for sexual assault victims, the appointment of a third of the Supreme Court including credibly accused attempted rapist Bret Kavanaugh, a botched response to the COVID-19 pandemic that caused the death of hundreds of thousands of Americans, and encouraging the insurrection attempt at the Capitol. Trump was impeached twice, an unenviable record for any President in American history, but both times saved from conviction by conservative Senators.

Fear Is a Path to the Dark Side

While Emperor Palpatine was able to use the Death Star and Stormtroopers to strike back against the Rebellion, conservatives have wielded an equally powerful weapon: moral panics. Originating in the work of Stanley Cohen, a moral panic is a response to a perceived threat stemming from new behavior that threatens existing social hierarchies.[4]

Cohen identified five stages of the process. First, "moral entrepreneurs," typically those at the top of the societal food chain, identify a behavior among the underclass that they find troubling. In almost every case, this behavior either undermines or exposes the social systems that perpetuate the moral entrepreneurs' power.[5] Second, they enlist the mass media and community members to spread the message and normalize the behavior as threatening.[6] This is accomplished largely by reducing those engaging in the objectionable behavior in simplified and symbolic terms. Third, once the threat has been identified, the entrepreneurs stoke social outrage against the behavior by exaggerating its potential destructive effects.[7] Fourth, having invented a villain, politicians and policymakers cast themselves as the heroes and put forth new legislation and policies designed, on their face, to combat the perceived problem. In reality, these actions typically do little to limit the behavior and often exacerbate the problem.[8] Finally, once society has granted the state the power to solve the manufactured problem, lasting social change is implemented that further cements the power hierarchies that maintain the moral entrepreneurs top positions.[9]

Each time the conservative empire struck back, they utilized a moral panic to do so. For example, Jim Crow laws relied on the moral panic of an alleged increased crime rate, playing on Southern Whites' fears that newly liberated Black people were violent savages seeking revenge for centuries of being enslaved. Reagan and the Moral Majority played on fears that the United States, which was never a Christian nation, was somehow becoming godless and overrun by hippies and women who wanted to mass-murder their so-called "unborn children." In reality, the American Christian opposition to abortion is younger than the McDonalds Happy Meal, as prior to the 1970s the general consensus among evangelicals was that fetuses did not have a soul.[10] Trump used similar moral panic techniques, claiming Democrats wanted to destroy the country's economic prosperity, permit sexual predators to assault girls in restrooms, allow terrorists to attack American soil, and put factory workers into unemployment.[11]

Start Wars

The events in Congress – detailed in the next section – where it became illegal for Pell grants to be given to prisoners did not occur in a vacuum. Instead, they were the outgrowth of the moral panic about criminals and the "undeserving poor" whose seeds were planted in the 1960s. Barry Goldwater was a Republican Senator from Arizona who famously stated that morality cannot be legislated.[12] This statement would prove ironic as he attempted to do just that in his failed election attempt against Johnson in 1964 where he became the first Presidential candidate to ever make law and order, a phrase now ubiquitous among the Republican Party, one of his campaign blanks. While Goldwater did not prevail in the election, his ideas that the President should be in the business of reducing crime did. Facing pressure from the public, Johnson declared the "War on Crime," a program that would become his legacy despite signing the Civil Rights Act and implementing his "Great Society" programs.[13] It seems Johnson took the "War" quite literally, proposing and passing the Law Enforcement Assistance Act that would begin the militarization of America's police force. The $30 million program, close to a quarter billion in modern dollars, bought bulletproof vests, armored vehicles, helicopters, assault rifles, and gas masks for police departments across the country. On his way out of office, Johnson signed the Omnibus Crime Control and Safe Streets Act, permanentizing the Department of Justice's influence on state law enforcement policy by increasing grant programs where the Department would provide funds to police departments for further equipment and training through the newly created Office of Law Enforcement Assistance.[14] Johnson's other war, the "War on Poverty," never received anywhere near the level of financial support the "War on Crime" did.

The 1968 election of Richard Nixon would forever alter the American political landscape. Despite being the incumbent, Johnson dropped out of the primary race after narrowly winning the New Hampshire primary. Following the assassination of Robert Kennedy, Johnson's Vice President Hubert Humphrey became the Democratic candidate. While Nixon would ultimately prevail, the entrance of infamous racist and segregation proponent George Wallace would inform Nixon's political strategy. Up until 1964, the South had universally favored Democrats when they voted for Goldwater who publicly opposed civil rights legislation and advocated for "tough on crime" policies.[15] As the Democratic Party went toward the left, save for the Dixiecrats, the racist white majority of the former Confederacy searched for new leadership. Taking his cues from Goldwater, Nixon implemented his Southern Strategy for the first time in 1968, appealing to white fears of Black equality and promoting increased police action in order to try to carry the South. As Fairclough put it,

> Nixon shrewdly exploited the racial fears and resentments that Wallace had whipped up. Promising law and order, courting Senator Strom Thurmond of South Carolina, vowing to appoint a Southern conservative to the Supreme Court, and vociferously denouncing the busing of children to promote school integration.[16]

Nixon was thwarted in this attempt by the even more racist George Wallace, who achieved national notoriety for standing in the doorway at the University of Alabama in a theatric attempt to prevent desegregation by blocking the first Black students from entering, carried Arkansas, Louisiana, Mississippi, Alabama, and Georgia.[17] With Wallace out of the picture in 1972, Nixon's Southern Strategy became a resounding success as he won every state but Massachusetts. Republicans would continue to use this strategy, portraying themselves as the party of law and order and Democrats as permissive liberals, to make gains within Congress and the White House.[18] The single exception to this was the election of one-term President Jimmy Carter, who is the only Democrat to win the entire South since Goldwater and to win Alabama, Mississippi, South Carolina, or Texas since Nixon's reelection. In fact, it was likely Gerald Ford's pardon of Richard Nixon, which was wildly unpopular and cut against the law and order image, that precipitated his loss to Carter. Carter's single four years in office was sandwiched between two decades of Republican control of the White House amidst four Presidents: Nixon, Ford, Ronald Reagan, and George H.W. Bush,

While in office, Republican Presidents continued the Southern Strategy, creating a moral panic regarding violent crime and drug use and positioning themselves rhetorically as the only heroes standing between the nation and mass chaos. In 1971, Nixon declared the "War on Drugs" as a companion to the "War on Crime." Having previously signed the Controlled Substances Act in 1970 which created the five schedules for drugs still utilized today, Nixon created the Drug Enforcement Agency as the country's first federal police force dedicated to prosecuting drug crimes.[19] As his domestic policy chief, John Ehrlichman, would reveal in 1994, the "War on Drugs" was perfectly aligned with Nixon's Southern Strategy moral panic. As noted previously, moral panics manufacture villains to permit those in power to implement policies that further their power. For Nixon, the "War on Drugs" was actually, according to Ehrlichman, a War on "the anti-war Left and Black people."[20] *Harper* magazine quoted Ehrlichman's interview with journalist Dan Baum where he stated

> We knew we couldn't make it illegal to be either against the war or Black, but by getting the public to associate the hippies with marijuana and Blacks with heroin, and then criminalizing both heavily, we could disrupt those communities. We could arrest their leaders, raid their homes, break up their meetings, and vilify them night after night on the evening news. Did we know we were lying about the drugs? Of course, we did.[21]

While Carter would actually campaign on marijuana decriminalization, Reagan would once again take up the mantle of the War on Drugs.

Together with First Lady Nancy Reagan, he launched the "Just Say No" campaign in 1982. The campaign enlisted popular television shows like *Punky Brewster, Diff'rent Strokes,* and *Dynasty* as well as organizations like the Girl Scouts of America to spread its message. While not officially a government program, D.A.R.E. (Drug Abuse Resistance Education), a highly ineffectual and criticized program aimed at teaching schoolchildren to resist drugs, was initiated a year later in 1983.[22] In 1986, Reagan signed the Anti-Drug Abuse Act, which replaced the 1952 Boggs Act – which was also drug prohibition – as the nation's only federal mandatory minimum sentencing legislation.[23] Hearkening back to Nixon's original racist policies, the law was rightfully criticized for targeting Black drug users far more than whites. Crack cocaine, most often used by Black Americans, carried a much steeper penalty than the powdered cocaine whites regularly used. While it took 500 grams of powdered cocaine to trigger a mandatory five-year sentence, a mere 5 grams of crack would merit the same minimum sentence.[24]

George H.W. Bush would continue the artificial War on Drugs. Despite crack usage being down in 1989, the elder Bush wanted a spectacle and demanded the DEA procure drugs sold across the street from the White House in Lafayette Park. Of course, there were very few drug deals happening in the prominent area typically swarming with tourists and Secret Service, so the DEA manipulated 19-year-old high school student Keith Jackson into doing the deed. While the DEA was aware that Jackson sold crack in his neighborhood, he had never been to Lafayette Park and didn't know where the White House was until one of the undercover DEA agents told him to meet them there to sell his illegal wares. During Bush's first televised Presidential address, he held up the baggie of crack and sought to alarm viewers by telling them it was purchased across the street from where he sat in the Oval Office. According to Bush, it could have just as easily been heroin or PCP, which is technically true since the DEA could have set up whatever type of dealer that the President wanted. After the speech, the DEA promptly arrested Jackson and charged him with the crime they asked him to commit. While he was ultimately acquitted on that charge, he was sentenced to 10 years in prison on two other charges, a sentence required by the law Reagan had signed. District Judge Stanley Sporkin, understandably enraged by the setup, encouraged Jackson to ask Bush to commute his sentence, a request Bush refused.

Outside of his actions on drugs, Bush also continued the "War on Crime." In his 1988 election against Democrat Michael Dukakis, Bush used the story of William "Willie" Horton as a continual talking point. When Dukakis was governor of Massachusetts, he vetoed an amendment to the state's furlough program that would have prevented the temporary releases of prisoners serving time for first-degree murder. One such prisoner was Horton who was granted a furlough in June 1986 and did not return to prison afterward. Ten months later, he raped a woman multiple times after attacking and tying up her fiancé. Bush's campaign seized on this controversy, bringing it up so often that campaign manager Lee Atwater once quipped that he hoped people would wonder if Horton was Dukakis' running mate.[25] The National Security Political Action Committee produced a now infamous attack ad, entitled "Weekend Passes," where they used Horton's story to claim Dukakis was soft on crime, while positioning Bush as the hero who supported the death penalty for murderers instead of weekend passes. While the Bush campaign technically did not produce the ad, they certainly benefited from it and soon released their own smear campaign called "Revolving Door" which likewise attacked the furlough program. In response, rather than defend his stance on the rehabilitation of prisoners, Dukakis attempted to play the Republican's "tough on crime" game by launching his own ad about a heroin dealer who raped and killed a pregnant mother after escaping from a halfway house.[26] While this was too little, too late for Dukakis, who lost 49 of 50 states in the election, it laid the groundwork for future Democratic stances on crime.

With the social outrage from the "War on Drugs" and the "War on Crime" firmly entrenching Republican power, Democrats had a choice to make. If they ever wanted to regain power, they had to persuade at least some of the South to vote for them. Since the implementation of the Southern Strategy, two different Republicans, Nixon and Reagan, had a nearly clean sweep of electoral votes, each winning all but one state. They needed a champion, someone the South would get behind, and they found him in Arkansas.

A New Hope?

The man from a place called Hope, Bill Clinton, would become not only the new face of the Democratic Party, but the galvanizing force behind Democrats joining the "tough on crime" stance. A native Arkansan and the state's former governor, Clinton selected Al Gore of Tennessee as his running mate, breaking the long tradition of running

mates being from the North and South. In the election that would gain
Democrats control of the White House and both houses of Congress,
Clinton took several states of the former Confederacy including Ar-
kansas, Louisiana, Georgia, and Tennessee, the latter of which would
prove to be the tipping point state. Additionally, he made significant
gains in the Southern states he did not win, narrowly losing North
Carolina by 0.79%, Florida by 1.89%, and even Bush's home state of
Texas by 3.48%.

In short, Clinton successfully coopted the Republican's Southern
Strategy and beat them at their own game. This phenomenon was
readily acknowledged by the media. A 1992 New York Times article
went so far as to open with the line:

> Gov. Bill Clinton took a page from the Republican playbook to-
> day, standing on the steps of City Hall here with uniformed police
> officers arrayed behind him as he denounced President Bush's re-
> cord on fighting crime.[27]

Adapting the Republican notion of "law and order" to his campaign's
"order and safety," Clinton railed against Bush for his alleged inaction
on crime prevention, claiming that he cared more for partisan politics
than keeping the streets safe. He claimed Bush refused to sign hand-
gun legislation and critiqued him for cutting $100 million from federal
funds for police departments, while emphasizing his commitment to a
program that would add more literal soldiers to the "War on Crime"
by creating a fast-track for former military to become cops.[28] No
longer was criminal justice in electoral politics about the differences
between rehabilitation and retribution. Instead, the Democrats and
Republicans began a contest of who could appear tougher on crime
and on criminals. Rather than bringing balance to the (police) force,
the Democratic rebellion had turned to the dark side.

The Tide Begins to Turn

While this massive political shift that gave the now quasi-Republican
Democrats control of the legislature and the White House, the roots
of the end of prison education began a few years before. In 1982, mid-
way through Reagan's first term, Congressman William Whitehurst, a
Republican from Virginia, introduced the first legislation to bar prisoners from receiving Pell Grants.[29] While the bill was defeated, similar legislation was introduced every year until the program's eventual
elimination in 1994.[30]

Opponents of prison education scored their first victory with the 1988 Anti-Drug Abuse Act signed by Reagan. In addition to establishing mandatory minimum sentences, it also made people with certain drug convictions ineligible for Pell funds, whether they were in prison or not.[31] The moral panic of the "War on Drugs" justified these actions. Drug users were the enemy, so the only public dollars spent on them should be for locking them up, not educating them. Once they found the public receptive to these tactics, legislators moved on to the next target: taking funding away from criminal students serving time for any offense.

In 1991, the year before Clinton was elected, Massachusetts Governor William Weld, perhaps having learned from his predecessor Dukakis' downfall, took a decidedly "tough on crime" stance. He called a press conference where he exclaimed:

> We've got to stop giving a free college education to prison inmates, or else the people who cannot afford to go to college are going to start committing crimes so they can get sent to prison to get a free education![32]

This would be the first time the "kids before cons" rhetoric was used, but in a rather unique way. Rather than claiming prisoners were somehow stealing Pell funds from law-abiding children, Weld hyperbolically suggested that children whose parents could not send them to college might be better off becoming felons if only for the allegedly free education. He would repeat this same claim that year on a segment of *60 Minutes* entitled "Prison U" and was not alone in making this outlandish assertion.[33] Maureen Donavan, the founder and president of Citizens Against an Unsafe Society, jumped into anti-prisoner advocacy after reading about Horton. The Massachusetts native, who had quarreled with Dukakis over the furlough program, stated on the *60 Minutes* segment that:

> you sell drugs, you murder someone, you rape someone, you go to prison and you get a free education. You hear kids saying now, "Well, you know, if I can't make it, you know, I can foul up and I'll go to prison and I'll get a free education."[34]

It is entirely doubtful that Donavan ever heard any kid say anything of the sort. The truth, however, matters little in moral panics. Prison college programs became the new villain, somehow luring innocent children to commit heinous murders and sex crimes in order to get their degrees paid for by the government. The solution, of course, was to eliminate prison college funding, lest it tempt little Johnny into becoming a rapist so that he could earn his Bachelor's in economics.

This argument remains the battle cry of the anti-prisoner education movement. In 2014, after New York Governor Andrew Cuomo announced a plan to use taxes of fund inmate education, a campaign entitled Kids Before Cons was launched by Assemblyman Steve McLaughlin.[35] The campaign featured a commercial accompanied by sad music where college students hold up paper signs denoting the tens of thousands of dollars they owe in student loans. Students call the prison funding proposal "stupid" and "insulting" and the ad ends with the narrator stating "We played by the rules, they broke the rules. We still have to pay for our college education, why do we have to pay for theirs too?"[36] Other campaign media feature pictures of t-shirts emblazoned with "SUNY RIKERS" and "ATTICA A&M" while comparing a stock photo of a multicultural group of young people with the caption "Studied hard. Worked Summer Jobs. Saved. Took out loans. All to pay for expensive college educations" to what appears to be a picture of a prisoner in a video game with the caption "Stole a car. Robbed a bank. Shot a bystander. Got a free education paid for by YOU." Despite this low-budget effort to convince New Yorkers that their taxes were going to pay for what appears to be a villain from the *Grand Theft Auto* video game series to go to college, the campaign drew public outcry and Cuomo withdrew his proposal roughly a month after announcing it. US Representative Steve Collins, a Republican also from New York, used the same rhetoric in 2015 when he authored the Kids Before Cons Act to prohibit Obama's Second Chance Pell program. Unlike the state campaign, that bill died in committee.

Four months after the airing of "Prison U," North Carolina Senator Jesse Helms, who had defected from the Democrats to become a Republican in 1970 after voting against the Civil Rights Act and the Voting Rights Act, attempted to enact Weld and Donovan's baseless arguments into law. Helms introduced an amendment initially to the appropriations bill and later to the Higher Education Reauthorization Act that would prevent any state or federal inmate from receiving Pell funds. He was clearly confident based on the 1988 legislation's prohibition for those with drug convictions, citing it in a speech on the floor of the Senate that concluded with "I see no reason why other criminals, including murderers, should be treated any better."[37] In 1992, the Senate passed the bill and a companion amendment offered in the House by Missouri Republican Thomas Coleman and Tennessee Democrat Bart Gordon was passed overwhelmingly with a vote of

351–369. Perhaps laying the foundation for the Democrat adoption of the Southern Strategy with Clinton's election, Gordon's sponsorship of the amendment would be one of the first times a modern Democrat embraced the "tough on crime" ethos. Prison education funding would narrowly survive this attack, as the reconciliation conference between the House and Senate versions of the bills was reduce the Pell ban from all inmates to prisoners on death row or serving life sentences. Gordon, however, would become a key player in the eventual death of prison Pell grant funding.

The Empire Strikes

Perhaps the most controversial criminal justice legislation of the modern era, except perhaps the USA Patriot Act, is the 1994 Violent Crime Control and Law Enforcement Act. Its Senate author and current President of the United States Joe Biden bragged after its passage that the Democrats were proud of the "60 new death penalties," "70 enhanced penalties," "100,000 cops," and "125,000 new state prison cells" that the law provided. The law, which contained everything from "three strikes policies" to a decade assault weapons ban to the first Violence Against Women Act, was a strategic attempt by the New Democrats, led by Biden and Clinton, "to wrestle the issue of crime away from Republicans."[38]

For Biden, this was nothing new. He led the charge and sponsored previous bills that were aimed at increasing criminal penalties within the "War on Drugs." The 1986 Comprehensive Control Act, which he pushed for along with Republican and notorious racist Strom Thurmond, expanded federal drug trafficking sentences and civil asset forfeiture. He sponsored the 1986 Anti-Drug Abuse Act, that he partly authored, which contained the infamous disparity of punishments for crack and powdered cocaine. He also co-sponsored the 1988 Anti-Drug Abuse Act which increased penalties for drug possession and trafficking as well as forming the Office of National Drug Control Policy. Even Bush wasn't tough enough on crime for Biden, who publicly criticized the President's War on Drugs plan in 1989, stating that it "doesn't include enough police officers to catch the violent thugs, not enough prosecutors to convict them, not enough judges to sentence them, and not enough prison cells to put them away for a long time."[39]

Eliminating prison education funding, however, was not part of Biden's original draft of the bill. While he did not author the amendment which precluded it, he did openly acknowledge that he worked to pass it. Prior to freshman Senator and Texas Republican Kay Bailey Hutchison's introduction of the amendment on November 16, 1993, Biden stated:

> While she is preparing to make her case, I have been trying to clear her amendment on our side. I may be able to save her a considerable amount of time. The last Democrat who had an objection to her amendment has now agreed that I can accept the amendment.[40]

After Republican Senate Minority leader Orrin Hatch announced that the GOP also found the amendment acceptable, Biden noted that he would call for unanimous consent to immediately vote on it after her speech, which he did. Ironically, Pell grants for prisoners would be resurrected two decades later by Biden's running mate, President Barack Obama, in 2015.

First Degree for Committing First-Degree

While Hutchison would author the Senate amendment that would pass largely without debate on the floor of the Senate, the House version was for more contentious. Much like the 1992 attempt, the news media had a significant role in shaping public discourse surrounding Pell grants for prisoners. One day prior to the introduction of the House version of the amendment, *Dateline* aired a special called "Society's Debt?" which, taking a cue from Hutchison's comments, set the stage for the newest rhetorical version of the "think about the children" argument. Where *60 Minites* had fallaciously argued that young adults would be enticed to commit crimes by the promise of a free degree behind bars, *Dateline* took a decidedly different angle: pitting "deserving young students" who "can't afford to go to college" against incarcerated students, "the lucky ones with no income and plenty of time to study" in a zero sum game.[41] The segment interviewed a college student who complained that he had to work at a part-time job to pay his tuition while prison students had cable television, weight rooms, and other luxuries while they earned their allegedly free degrees. Additionally, a father of a murdered teen expressed his anger at prison education, echoing pieces of the *60 Minutes* argument, that prisoners were rewarded for their crimes with a degree while his son would never get to attend college. He stated "and we're saying to him, 'Thank you very much for killing somebody. We're going to give you a college education.'"

In her prepared remarks that were added to the Congressional Record, but not spoken on the Senate floor, Hutchison echoed this same allegation of unfairness, claiming that prisoners with:

> ...sentences for offenses like carjacking, armed robbery, rape, and arson received as much as $200 million in Pell funds, courtesy of the American taxpayer. This is not right. This is not fair to the more than 1 million eligible students who were denied Pell grants last year because there was not enough money in the program. It is not fair to the millions of parents who work and pay taxes, and then must scrape and save and often borrow to finance their children's educations.[42]

One could almost picture an American flag waving behind Hutchison as they read her written argument, that she advocated for

> stretching every possible dollar for those young people who stay out of trouble, study hard, and deserve a chance to further their education, fair to working Americans who pay their taxes and do without in order that their children will have advantages they never had: a better education, more opportunities, a better future.[43]

For Hutchison, it was patently unfair that existing laws "put convicts at the head of the line for college financial aid, crowding out law-abiding citizens."[44] As an example, Hutchison mentioned a police officer who was frustrated his daughter did not receive a Pell grant, but inmates did.

The Truth Matters Little

This same line of argumentation was echoed in the House. Gordon, who introduced the amendment, repeated the claim that prisoners were getting $200 million yearly in Pell funds "squeezing out thousands of traditional students."[45] Echoing Hutchison's comments, Gordon stated "law-abiding students have every right to be outraged when a Pell grant for a policeman's child is cut but a criminal that the officer sends to prison can still get a big check."[46] The same sentiment was argued by Representative Jack Fields of Texas, notably the only Republican involved in the House debate, where he stated "Every dollar in Pell grant funds obtained by prisoners means that fewer law-abiding students who need help in meeting their college costs are eligible for that assistance."[47] Tim Holden, a Pennsylvania Democrat, quoted at length from a letter from one of his constituents:

> Where is an average, hard-working student who wants to make something of herself and get somewhere in life supposed to turn for help? Over the years we have told our daughter, "Keep your nose clean, stay out of trouble. If you have a police record, you will never get into college." My daughter has listened, but where has it gotten her? She reads about prisoners getting Pell grants and free college educations. What does this tell her? It tells her: If she was sitting in jail she would get a free education. Just where does a hard-working normal honor student involved in many extracurricular activities not only in school but also in the community go for help? The prisoner is rewarded with a free education. The average honor student is penalized because she tried to save money for college and she is penalized because she stayed out of trouble. Who can justify all of this?[48]

For the proponents of Pell legislation, there was an easy answer to the choice. Choose the innocent law-abiding children over the evil criminals. The truth, however, that matters little if at all in moral panics is that the two sides were never in opposition in the first place.

Hutchison and Gordon claimed that prisoners were receiving $200 million in Pell grants yearly. This was patently false. In 1993, there were only 38,000 incarcerated students nationwide.[49] Of that, only 80%, 30,000, received Pell funds.[50] Since Pell grants in the 1990s averaged $1,400 per student – a fact that the proponents of the ban admitted to on the floor of Congress – this means the actual amount all prison students received that year was no more than $42 million, about 80% less than the $200 million Hutchison and Gordon claimed. Additionally, prisoners were not, as the legislators claimed, pushing any law-abiding citizen out of the way. Pell grants are a quasi-entitlement program. Every eligible person who applies for one receives it and the amount received is divided from the pool of funds and distributed up to the capped amount.[51] In fact, the only way to not receive Pell funds is not to qualify because your family makes too much money – which was the case with the police officer Hutchison mentioned. His daughter was not denied Pell funds because they went to prisoners, but because he made more than $4,000 a year above the maximum income that a family can make and be eligible for a Pell grant.[52] Hutchison also failed to mention that the police officer's daughter could receive $30,000 in forgivable Perkins Loans by virtue of her father's profession, 10 times the amount a prisoner would receive to earn an Associate's degree behind bars.[53] No person was or could ever be denied a Pell grant because prisoners received them. All 1.5 million men and women currently incarcerated could receive Pell grants and it would not prevent, nor has it ever prevented, a single eligible recipient from being awarded Pell money.

That said, 1.5 million prisoners did not receive Pell grants the year funds were removed, only 30,000 did. According to the Department of Education, they accounted for 0.6% of funding in 1994, the year that Congress made them ineligible for Pell grants.[54] This paltry amount, six tenths of 1% of the Pell budget, if evenly distributed would mean each recipient would get less than an additional $5 a semester. The price of denying 30,000 incarcerated students the means to go to school would barely pay for an extra latte each semester.

The truly damning aspect of this situation is that Hutchison, Gordon, and the other legislators who pushed these amendments through were aware of these facts. In the debate in the House, Democrat Representative Albert Wynn of Maryland repeatedly informed them that "Prisoners only utilize one half of 1% of Pell grant funding" which "does not constitute $200 million as has been suggested but, rather, I submit, only $35 million out of a $6.3 billion program."[55] He further rebutted the false claims that people were being denied because prisoners received Pell grants, stating:

> It has been suggested that law-abiding students are denied Pell grants because persons incarcerated are getting Pell grants. That is not true. The administration's statement clearly indicates that the availability of Pell grants to prisoners has no effect on the availability of Pell grants to law-abiding students. By law, all eligible students who apply for Pell grants receive them.[56]

Congress, however, did not have to take Wynn's word for it. These same facts had been argued against the prior attempt at passing this same legislation in 1991 by Senator Claiborne Pell. The name is no coincidence, he was literally the person Pell grants were named after. Congress ignored Wynn, the facts, and the person for whom the Pell grant program was named in order to pass their legislation.

"No More Studies"

The proponents of banning Pell grants for prisoners were not only averse to existing facts, they also wanted nothing to do with research into the topic. During the floor debate in the House, Fields infamously exclaimed:

> No more studies, no more delays. It is a straightforward, simple amendment. If you oppose Pell grants for prisoners, you should vote for the Gordon-Holden-Fields amendment...
>
> We do not need any more studies. We need more higher education funds for our constituents' sons and daughters who are struggling to pay for their children's college expenses. Our constituents already pay to feed, house, clothe and rehabilitate prisoners. Their sons and daughters shouldn't have to do without so that incarcerated prisoners can use Pell grant funds to go to college.[57]

The studies Fields wanted no more of were those that demonstrated that prison education reduces recidivism. This effect was well known to Congress, as Wynn pointed out, "National statistics indicate that while the national recidivism rate is between 60 and 65% for those prisoners that partake of post-secondary education under this program, the recidivism rate is only 10 to 30 percent."[58] The same data set used in the infamous Martinson Report in 1974 was used in another published study in 1975, in which Martinson was a co-author, that reported positive outcomes for 48% of prisoner rehabilitation programs.[59] Martinson himself revised his initial findings five years later, noting that certain programs did, in fact, effectively rehabilitate prisoners.[60]

As has been repeated multiple times, facts matter little in moral panics. However, what Fields argued was not only to ignore existing facts, but that we did not need more studies to discover more of them. Instead of following the data, the proponents of eliminating Pell grants stuck to their uninformed ideas, arguing not with facts but with folksy analogies. In the 1992 debates, the 1994 debates, and an op-ed in USA Today, Gordon used the same trope:

> Just because one blind hog may occasionally find an acorn does not mean many other blind hogs will. The same principle applies to giving Federal Pell grants to prisoners. Certainly there is an occasional success story, but when virtually every prisoner in America is eligible for Pell grants, national priorities and taxpayers lose.[61]

Comparing inmates to animals, Gordon was successfully able to dismiss studies showing the effectiveness of prison education programs as simple luck or happenstance. In his mind, criminals were, after all, evil by nature and their success was no reason to spend taxpayer's dollars. Why was it, at the end of the 20th century, that Gordon was able to successfully make his case by comparing prisoners to animals? The answer lies in the media.

Notes

1 Bob Anderson, "Homer vs. the eighteenth amendment," in *The Simpsons* (20th Century FOX, 1997).
2 C Vann Woodward, *Reunion and reaction: The compromise of 1877 and the end of reconstruction* (New York: Oxford University Press, 1991).
3 Michelle Alexander, *The new Jim Crow: Mass incarceration in the age of colorblindness* (New York: The New Press, 2012).
4 Stanley Cohen, *Folk devils and moral panics: The creation of the mods and rockers* (London: Psychology Press, 2002).
5 Cohen, *Folk devils and moral panics.*
6 Cohen, *Folk devils and moral panics.*
7 Cohen, *Folk devils and moral panics.*
8 Cohen, *Folk devils and moral panics.*
9 Cohen, *Folk devils and moral panics.*
10 Jonathan Dudley, *Broken words: The abuse of science and faith in American politics* (New York: Crown, 2011).
11 Jennifer Mercieca, *Demagogue for president: The rhetorical genius of Donald Trump* (College Station: Texas A&M University Press, 2020).
12 Ted Gest, *Crime & politics: Big government's erratic campaign for law and order* (New York: Oxford University Press on Demand, 2003).
13 Elizabeth Hinton, "Why we should reconsider the war on crime," *TIME*, 2015, https://time.com/3746059/war-on-crime-history/.
14 William J Chambliss, *Power, politics and crime* (New York: Westview Press, 2001).
15 Gest, *Crime & politics.*
16 Adam Fairclough, *Better day coming: Blacks and equality, 1890-2000* (New York:Penguin, 2001), 323.
17 E Culpepper Clark, *The schoolhouse door: Segregation's last stand at the university of Alabama* (New York: Oxford University Press, 1995).
18 Joseph A Aistrup, *The southern strategy revisited: Republican top-down advancement in the South* (Lexington: University Press of Kentucky, 2014).
19 Carlos A Pérez Ricart, "The role of the DEA in the emergence of the field of anti-narcotics policing in Latin America," *Global Governance: A Review of Multilateralism and International Organizations* 24, no. 2 (2018): 169–92.
20 Dan Baum, "Legalize it all," *Harper's Magazine* 24 (2016): 22.
21 Baum, "Legalize it all," 22.
22 Steven L West and Keri K O'Neal, "Project DARE outcome effectiveness revisited," *American Journal of Public Health* 94, no. 6 (2004): 1027–29.
23 Alyssa L Beaver, "Getting a fix on cocaine sentencing policy: reforming the sentencing scheme of the anti-drug abuse act of 1986," *Fordham Law Review* 78 (2009): 2531–75.
24 Beaver, "Getting a fix on cocaine sentencing policy."

25 David C Anderson and Catherine Enberg, "Crime and the politics of hysteria: How the Willie Horton story changed American justice," *Journal of Contemporary Criminal Justice* 11, no. 4 (1995): 298–300.
26 Anderson and Enberg, "Crime and the politics of hysteria."
27 Gwen Ifill, "The 1992 campaign: The democrats; Clinton, in Houston speech, assails Bush on crime issue," *The New York Times* 1992, A, 13.
28 Ifill, "The 1992 campaign," 13.
29 Jon Marc Taylor, "Pell grants for prisoners: Why should we care?" *Journal of Prisoners on Prisons* 17, no. 1 (2008): 18–29.
30 Charles BA Ubah, "Abolition of Pell Grants for higher education of prisoners: Examining antecedents and consequences," *Journal of Offender Rehabilitation* 39, no. 2 (2004): 73–85 .
31 Joshua Page, "Eliminating the enemy: The import of denying prisoners access to higher education in Clinton's America," *Punishment & Society* 6, no. 4 (2004): 357–78.
32 James Gilligan, *Violence in California prisons: A proposal for research into patterns and cures* (Sacramento: Senate Publications, 2000), 11.
33 Gail Eisen, "Prison U," in *60 Minutes* (New York: CBS, 1991).
34 Eisen, "Prison U."
35 Casey Seiler, "'Kids before cons' petition illustration is, uh, colorful," *Times Union* 2014, https://blog.timesunion.com/capitol/archives/206723/kids-before-cons-petition-illustration-is-uh-colorful/.
36 NY RACC, "Kids before cons," (YouTube, 2014), https://www.youtube.com/watch?v=Fdy10zEBbl1k.
37 Seiler, "'Kids before cons' petition illustration is, uh, colorful."
38 German Lopez, "The controversial 1994 crime law that Joe Biden helped write, explained," *Vox* (Microsoft News) 2020, https://www.msn.com/en-us/news/politics/the-controversial-1994-crime-law-that-joe-biden-helped-write-explained/ar-BB19xrKq.
39 Lopez, "The controversial 1994 crime law that Joe Biden helped write, explained."
40 U.S. Congress, Senate-Tuesday, November 16, 1993 S29449 (Congressional Record 1993).
41 Dateline, "Society's debt?," in *Dateline* (New York: NBC, 1994).
42 U.S. Congress, Short Senate-Tuesday, November 16, 1993 S29449.
43 U.S. Congress, Short Senate-Tuesday, November 16, 1993 S29449.
44 U.S. Congress, Short Senate-Tuesday, November 16, 1993 S29449.
45 U.S. Congress, House Of Representatives-Wednesday, April 20, 1994 H7948 (Congressional Record 1994).
46 U.S. Congress, Short House Of Representatives-Wednesday, April 20, 1994 H7948.
47 U.S. Congress, Short House Of Representatives-Wednesday, April 20, 1994 H7949.
48 U.S. Congress, Short House Of Representatives-Wednesday, April 20, 1994 H7949.
49 Jamie Lillis, "Prison education programs reduced," *Corrections Compendium* 19, no. 3 (1994): 1–4.
50 Jon Marc Taylor, "Pell grants for prisoners part deux: It's déja vu all over again," *Journal of Prisoners on Prisons* 8, no. 1 (1997): 1–11.
51 Taylor, "Pell Grants for prisoners part deux."
52 Taylor, "Pell Grants for prisoners part deux."

53 Taylor, "Pell Grants for prisoners part deux."
54 U.S. Department of Education, Request for 1993–1994 federal Pell Grant data – revised statistics, (Washington, D.C. 1994).
55 U.S. Congress, Short House Of Representatives-Wednesday, April 20, 1994 H7949.
56 U.S. Congress, Short House Of Representatives-Wednesday, April 20, 1994 H7949-50.
57 U.S. Congress, Short House Of Representatives-Wednesday, April 20, 1994 H7949.
58 U.S. Congress, Short House Of Representatives-Wednesday, April 20, 1994 H7948.
59 Douglas S Lipton, Robert Martinson, and Judith Wilks, *The effectiveness of correctional treatment: A survey of treatment evaluation studies* (New York:Greenwood, 1975).
60 Michael Welch, *Corrections: A critical approach* (London: Routledge, 2013).
61 U.S. Congress, Short House Of Representatives-Wednesday, April 20, 1994 H7948.

References

Aistrup, Joseph A. *The Southern Strategy Revisited: Republican Top-Down Advancement in the South.* Lexington, KY: University Press of Kentucky, 2014.

Alexander, Michelle. *The New Jim Crow: Mass Incarceration in the Age of Colorblindness.* New York: The New Press, 2012.

Anderson, Bob. "Homer Vs. The Eighteenth Amendment." In *The Simpsons*, 20th Century FOX, 1997.

Anderson, David C, and Catherine Enberg. "Crime and the Politics of Hysteria: How the Willie Horton Story Changed American Justice." *Journal of Contemporary Criminal Justice* 11, no. 4 (1995): 298–300.

Baum, Dan. "Legalize It All." *Harper's Magazine* 24 (2016): 22–32.

Beaver, Alyssa L. "Getting a Fix on Cocaine Sentencing Policy: Reforming the Sentencing Scheme of the Anti-Drug Abuse Act of 1986." *Fordham Law Review*, 78 (2009): 2531–75.

Chambliss, William J. *Power, Politics and Crime.* New York: Westview Press, 2001.

Clark, E Culpepper. *The Schoolhouse Door: Segregation's Last Stand at the University of Alabama.* New York: Oxford University Press, 1995.

Cohen, Stanley. *Folk Devils and Moral Panics: The Creation of the Mods and Rockers.* London: Psychology Press, 2002.

Dateline. "Society's Debt?" In *Dateline.* New York: NBC, 1994.

Dudley, Jonathan. *Broken Words: The Abuse of Science and Faith in American Politics.* New York: Crown, 2011.

Eisen, Gail. "Prison U." In *60 Minutes.* New York: CBS, 1991.

Fairclough, Adam. *Better Day Coming: Blacks and Equality, 1890–2000.* New York: Penguin, 2001.

Gest, Ted. *Crime & Politics: Big Government's Erratic Campaign for Law and Order.* New York: Oxford University Press on Demand, 2003.

Gilligan, James. *Violence in California Prisons: A Proposal for Research into Patterns and Cures.* Sacramento: Senate Publications, 2000.

Hinton, Elizabeth. "Why We Should Reconsider the War on Crime." *TIME,* 2015. https://time.com/3746059/war-on-crime-history/.

Ifill, Gwen. "The 1992 Campaign: The Democrats; Clinton, in Houston Speech, Assails Bush on Crime Issue." *The New York Times,* 1992, A, 13.

Lillis, Jamie. "Prison Education Programs Reduced." *Corrections Compendium* 19, no. 3 (1994): 1–4.

Lipton, Douglas S, Robert Martinson, and Judith Wilks. *The Effectiveness of Correctional Treatment: A Survey of Treatment Evaluation Studies.* New York: Greenwood, 1975.

Lopez, German. "The Controversial 1994 Crime Law That Joe Biden Helped Write, Explained." *Vox* (Microsoft News), 2020. https://www.msn.com/en-us/news/politics/the-controversial-1994-crime-law-that-joe-biden-helped-write-explained/ar-BB19xrKq.

Mercieca, Jennifer. *Demagogue for President: The Rhetorical Genius of Donald Trump.* College Station, TX: Texas A&M University Press, 2020.

Page, Joshua. "Eliminating the Enemy: The Import of Denying Prisoners Access to Higher Education in Clinton's America." *Punishment & Society* 6, no. 4 (2004): 357–78.

RACC, NY. "Kids before cons." YouTube, 2014. https://www.youtube.com/watch?v=Fdyl0zEBblk.

Ricart, Carlos A Pérez. "The Role of the Dea in the Emergence of the Field of Anti-Narcotics Policing in Latin America." *Global Governance: A Review of Multilateralism and International Organizations* 24, no. 2 (2018): 169–92.

Seiler, Casey. "'Kids before Cons' Petition Illustration Is, Uh, Colorful." *Times Union,* 2014. https://blog.timesunion.com/capitol/archives/206723/kids-before-cons-petition-illustration-is-uh-colorful/.

Taylor, Jon Marc. "Pell Grants for Prisoners Part Deux: It's Déja Vu All over Again." *Journal of Prisoners on Prisons* 8, no. 1 (1997): 1–11.

———. "Pell Grants for Prisoners: Why Should We Care?" *Journal of Prisoners on Prisons* 17, no. 1 (2008): 18–29.

U.S. Congress. *House of Representatives-Wednesday, April 20, 1994* Congressional Record, 1994.

———. *Senate-Tuesday, November 16, 1993* Congressional Record, 1993.

U.S. Department of Education. *Request for 1993–1994 Federal Pell Grant Data – Revised Statistics.* Washington, DC, 1994.

Ubah, Charles BA. "Abolition of Pell Grants for Higher Education of Prisoners: Examining Antecedents and Consequences." *Journal of Offender Rehabilitation* 39, no. 2 (2004): 73–85.

Welch, Michael. *Corrections: A Critical Approach.* London: Routledge, 2013.

West, Steven L, and Keri K O'Neal. "Project Dare Outcome Effectiveness Revisited." *American Journal of Public Health* 94, no. 6 (2004): 1027–29.

Woodward, C Vann. *Reunion and Reaction: The Compromise of 1877 and the End of Reconstruction.* New York: Oxford University Press, 1991.

3 Shawshank Irredeemable

In the popular film *Ant-Man*, main character Scott Lang (played by Paul Rudd) is released from the notorious San Quentin prison after serving three years for grand larceny.[1] When his friend and former cellmate Luis, actor Michael Peña, asks him where he plans to find a job, Lang remarked that he has a master's degree in Electrical Engineering and has no plans to continue breaking the law. The next scene shows Lang working and being summarily fired from popular ice cream chain *Baskin-Robbins*. In the latter part of the scene after Lang noted that the company had found out about his time in prison, the manager remarked "Baskin-Robbins always finds out." Despite the manager's emphasis and indeed enthusiasm about Lang, he is forced by company policy to terminate him.

This scene is meaningful for several reasons. It is one of the few accurate representations in media of the struggle former prisoners endure to reintegrate into society. Beyond that, it highlights the effect mediated perceptions have on individuals in their response to former prisoners. It is highly unlikely that the executives or human resources officers at *Baskin-Robbins* have ever met a former prisoner, yet the company not only has a policy prohibiting the employment of felons but unashamedly permitted the film to highlight it. *Baskin-Robbins* would never have a racist hiring policy and they would have likely sued Marvel if the film had claimed they did. In contrast, when the discrimination is against former prisoners, the company was more than happy to allow their name and image to be used in what is presented as a comical moment within the film. These policies come into place and are made socially acceptable through the mediated depictions of criminals, leading to real world effects which not only dehumanize former prisoners but further the problems of crime through recidivism.

Furthermore, it is this same mediated depiction of prisoners which informed the minds of the American public that Gordon was appealing

DOI: 10.4324/9781003189947-3

to when he compared inmates to "blind hogs." In any rhetorical situation, knowing the mindset of one's audience is crucial in engaging them with a persuasive message.[2] Gordon and his colleagues were well-aware that they were playing to a television audience. Created in 1979, C-SPAN is a public network that broadcasts Congressional and other government proceedings. By the time the crime bill came up for debate, over 70 million households had access to watch the arguments unfold. While only a fraction were watching live, Congress was aware that it was a significant number. Republican Representative Bob Dornan, for instance, noted that there were "1.5 million folks watching" the debate over the bill.[3] To amass political power, Gordon and the others had to both understand the mind of the audience they were performing for and meet their expectations. Therefore, to understand why Gordon's appeal was successful, the audience's perception of prisoners and criminals, almost exclusively formed by media, must be examined.

How Media Portrays Prisoners[4]

Prisons purposefully exist, in both location and design, in a manner designed to hide them and their occupants from the public eye. From being placed in unpopulated areas to the stone walls and razor-wire fences to heavy restrictions as to who can enter, prisons are in every way what Goffman termed a total institution.[5] As a result of these factors, "the prison is a closed milieu known to relatively few people, but about which there is much fascination and supposition within the wider population."[6] Despite this fascination, the public often lacks the means and the desire to enter a prison. Instead, they form their ideas and impressions of prisoners through their media consumption. Wilson argued that "ultimately when we present an image of prison we shape the public's expectation about what prison is like, and what happens inside, of who prisoners are and what they have done."[7] Further complicating this issue is that the public typically does not get their images of prisoners from journalists, as it is a rare occurrence for news media to include images of prisoners.[8] In the rare times prisoners get news coverage, it consists of almost entirely extremely negative events including riots and escapes.[9] Lacking any substantive coverage of the penal system by journalists, the public fills this void through popular media.

Viewers of television and films "use knowledge they obtain from the media to construct a picture of the world, an image of reality on which they base their actions."[10] In terms of prison, the primary source of this knowledge comes from fictional representations including films

and television programs.[11] Despite the plethora of entertainment op-
tions and topics available to the modern consumer, crime and violence
remains the most popular subject in media.[12] While this is a current
trend, it is by no means a new one. The American fascination with
criminal and penal depictions on media began in the early 20th century with films including *The Great Train Robbery* in 1903, *The Big
House* in 1930, and *Scar Face* in 1932.[13] A high demand in criminal
and prison themed films began in the 1940s and continued throughout
the century.[14] Crime and prison-centered television programs became
popular a decade later in the 1950s and they continue to be consumed
at high levels today.[15] In fact, a quarter of primetime television from
the 1960s through the 1990s had crime as a primary subject.[16] Likewise, prisoners and prisons became a popular subject for television
programs in the 1990s.[17]

There is an admitted gap in the literature concerning the media
effects of the portrayals of prisons and prisoner.[18] However, the limited scholarship which has addressed this issue found the portrayals
to be resoundingly negative. Cheliotis noted, "Prisons are most usu-
ally typecast either as dark institutions of perpetual horror and viru-
lent vandalism or idyllic holiday camps offering in-cell television and
gourmet cuisine on the back of taxpayers," while prisoners "are portrayed as degenerate beasts beyond redemption or undeserving laya-
bouts."[19] In an analysis of the prison-themed television program, *Oz*,
Rapping argued that the program "presents a vision of hell on earth in
which inmates are so depraved and vicious that no sane person could
possibly think they should ever again be let loose upon society."[20]
Even science fiction programs are not immune to this trend, as prisons
in the future resemble exponentially worse conditions. In a study of
prison images in such media, Nellis concluded their vision of the future demonstrated "prisons of the future will be hellish places, and...
there will surely be villains bad enough to justify their existence."[21]

Real Prisoners Can't Be Heroes

That is not to say that prison media does not have protagonists. The
protagonist inevitably fits the definition of a stock character within
prison media, the "young hero, who is either absolutely innocent or
at most guilty of a minor offense that does not warrant prison."[22]
The rest of the prisoners are "not normally viewed in anything other
than disparaging terms."[23] Rather than view all prisoners as human,
redemption "is reserved for the 'exceptional individual' while prisoners in general are seen as collectively incapable and undeserving of

rehabilitation."[24] Complicating this further is the continual use of the White Savior as a prisoner-hero. From Andy Dufrense in *The Shawshank Redemption* (portrayed by Tim Robbins) to Paul Crewe in *The Longest Yard* (portrayed by Burt Reynolds in 1974 and Adam Sandler in 2005) to Piper Chapman in *Orange Is The New Black* (portrayed by Taylor Schilling), the exceptional individual is almost always a white man or woman who shows their fellow inmates of color a better way to live. Therefore, the only individuals who are discursively produced as potential heroes are the – inevitably white – ones who do not belong in prison in the first place. The implication of this is the overwhelming majority of inmates are evil, therefore the prison system exists to justly punish them for their depraved ways.

The continual representation of all but a few prisoners as irredeemable deviants perpetuates the existing divide between the "civilised and the savage" but this divide is neither novel nor recent.[25] In Foucault's *Discipline and Punish*, he explained that at the dawn of the 19th-century public displays of punishment for criminals were quietly replaced by prisons as a more secretive forms of discipline. "It is ugly to be punishable, but there is no glory in punishing, hence the double system of protection that justice has set up between itself and the punishment it imposes."[26] While the state wished to enact the so-called justice of punishment on lawbreakers that the public demanded, it feared, and rightfully so, that its traditions of brutal public punishments would make the government seem less civil and more like the criminals it was punishing. By moving punishment outside of the public eye, the state was able to perpetuate the image of the prisoner as a scoundrel in need of punishment, while "justice is relieved of responsibility for it by a bureaucratic concealment of the penalty itself."[27] "This shift to supposedly more 'humane' forms of institutional correction was generally thought to remove flagrant barbarism and randomness, and to assert a credo of a 'civilised' modernity based on the rationalised rule of law."[28] This removal, however, did not quell the public's need to see the offender punished. Mason explained that "despite Foucault's genealogical account of the disappearance of the *ancien regime's* spectacle of punishment, of gallows and guillotine, visual spectacle persists in cinematic representations."[29]

In addition to being portrayed as morally unredeemable, the mediated image of prisoners and criminals also produces them as being hyper-violent. After World War II, crime films became increasingly violent as production companies shifted away from self-censorship and toward marketability.[30] Similarly, violence and resistance to authority are recurring themes in prison films.[31] The effect of this focus on violence is a play on the public's "fears by overstating the danger of criminal victimization, targeting weak and marginalized swathes of the population, criticizing the authorities for laxity, calling for more and harsher punitive measures, and blocking or neutralizing the imagery of human suffering thereby caused."[32] In short, fear sells. The media discursively produces criminals and prisoners as villains to be feared in order to attract viewers.

Media portrays prisoners en masse as justly punished villains because doing so "satisfies an almost primordial desire to view punishment as fundamental to the exercising of power."[33] As profit-minded businesses, media corporations reproduce the dominant ideological views of their audience in order to sell their product to consumers.[34] Cheatwood, in an analysis of 56 prison films released between 1929 and 1995, found that films reproduced the dominant views of each time period.[35] That is, the production companies framed prisoners in a way that they believe consumers want. In terms of media, frames "are the focus, a parameter or boundary, for discussing a particular event. Frames focus on what will be discussed, how it will be discussed, and above all, how it will not be discussed."[36] Given Tuchman's argument that existing frames are built upon prior frames, the 19th-century need to see prisoners punished is still evident within modern media.[37]

Not Changing Horses Mid-Streaming

While media has historically been unfavorable to prisoners, more recent movements within the entertainment industry have pushed for more inclusive programming aimed at changing the historic practices of racist, sexist, and homophobic portrayals. Given the advent of streaming services like *Netflix, Hulu,* and *Amazon Prime Video* replacing cable television subscriptions, I was interested to see if made-for-streaming prisoners differed from their made-for-TV counterparts.

Based on prior research, my research team identified instances of antisocial and negative behaviors in the following categories: violence, disrespect of authority, yelling/screaming, cursing, displays of anger/ aggression, and other miscellaneous anti-social behaviors like drug use and rule breaking. In total, 35 hours of available programming was analyzed. In total, 407 different instances of negative behavior were coded. This equated to more than 11 per hour or one new instance roughly every five minutes and ten seconds. The most commonly coded behaviors were forms of verbal aggression with violence and antisocial behaviors following closely behind. While this research is still in preliminary stages of analysis, it reveals a disturbing trend. Despite the change in platforms and the move toward equity for other groups, constructing prisoners as evil remains the norm with media production.

Media Shapes Public Ideas of Prisoners[38]

Leading anti-racism scholar, Joe Feagin, is perhaps best known for his development of the notion of the White Racial Frame.[39] According to his research, this worldview normalizes whiteness as the standard behavior, regularly insulating it from critique by making the evil actions of white people the sole responsibility rather than the racial culture. Simultaneously, it stereotypes and stigmatizes people of color as the Other, attributing negative qualities of individual members as evidence of the race itself being inferior. The White Racial Frame minimizes and ignores the effects of systemic racism which prop up white people and discriminate against people of color, conveniently pretending that the success of whites is earned through hard work rather than an unequal playing field. Feagin argues that media consumption is a primary vehicle by which the White Racial Frame is propagated, stating that it is "so institutionalized that all major media outlets operate out of some version of it."[40]

While carceral status is not a race, Feagin's analysis is useful for understanding the effects of media that continually portrays prisoners negatively in relation to the public's beliefs about and treatment of them. Through consumption of a diet of anti-prisoner media, the viewing public likewise develops its own Anti-Prisoner frame where it views those who have been convicted of crimes as wholly responsible for their actions while attributing their success to their good character instead of more privileged circumstances.

Social Learning and Cultivation Theories

Social learning theory stipulates that individuals acquire knowledge and belief through the process of observational learning.[41] Accordingly, humans observe behaviors performed by others, internalize them as acceptable, and begin to model them.[42] In terms of media, Bandura referred to "models presented mainly through television and films."[43] In my previous work, I provided examples of this type of modeling in relation to homophobia produced by a lack of LGBT-QIA+ characters on children's television programming.[44] Children viewing such media engaged in homophobia because they modeled the presented media's concepts that heterosexuality was the only normal state of existence.

Cultivation theory stems from the idea that long-term exposure to media works to cultivate certain attitudes, beliefs, and behaviors within viewers.[45] These include first-order beliefs about facts and second-order beliefs which encompass the ways in which we perceive particular issues. Cultivation functions through three different processes: mainstreaming, resonance, and substitution.

Mainstreaming occurs when viewers across various demographics adopt the same values promoted in media programming. A prime example of this in relation to criminality appeared in Gerbner's study on perceptions of crime.[46] Gerbner and his colleagues found mixed results between affluent and impoverished viewers who were light consumers of media. Those from higher economic classes who lived and worked in areas where they had little contact with crime did not view it as a serious issue, while those from lower economic classes who regularly encountered crime thought it to be much more problematic. This difference vanished among heavy viewers of media, as both affluent and impoverished viewers felt crime was a serious issue. Exposure to media, heavy-laden with messages about criminality, produced the same mainstreaming effect regardless of the viewer's circumstances.

Resonance and substitution have similar effects but work differently depending on the viewing population. Resonance occurs when media reflects and exaggerates the experiences a viewer has based on his or her personal experience. For instance, those respondents in Gerbner's study who lived in high crime areas experienced resonance when they saw their lived reality reflected in media portrayals of crime. The respondents living in low crime areas, however, had no experience to compare with the mediated version. Instead of resonance, they experienced substitution. Substitution is a phenomenon where a viewer lacks access to events or topics portrayed on media and uses their media consumption as a substituted basis of knowledge for them. Whether by resonating with experience or providing a substitute experience, media provides individuals with a source of knowledge on which to base their actions.

Cultivation theory works in conjunction with Social Learning theory in that through repeated experiences of social learning, viewers are thereby cultivated into the resultant performance of the modeled actions. However, both Cultivation and Social Learning rely on the viewer's perception that what they are seeing has some basis in reality. That is, if viewers perceive the content as unreal, it will likely neither produce ideas or learned behaviors.

(Un)reality TV

If prison media were simply a voyeuristic production that allowed viewers to live out their fantasies of justice, then it might be relatively harmless. Unfortunately, the effects of prisoner and criminal centered media serve to shape the public's perception of prisoners, prisons, criminals, and crime. The existing public perception of prisoners, "that they are the detritus of society and unworthy of civic concern," can be explained by understanding viewers often, consciously or unconsciously, perceive fictional prison media as real. Roughly half of prison films make the spurious claim to be representing reality or be based on a true story.[47] Given viewers' lack of personal knowledge of prisons and prisoners, they are therefore more likely to believe these claims of truth. Even prisoners themselves are not immune from these effects. Van den Bulck and Vandebosch reported that the prisoners they interviewed developed their initial views of carceral life from media, writing:

> the expectations of most of the inmates on entering the system were mainly based on television and movie images of prisons in the United States. They realized where they got their information from. They made explicit references to American audiovisual fiction. From it, they seemed to have been led to expect that the majority of inmates would be convicted of very serious crimes, that the experienced inmates would subject newcomers to an initiation ritual and that rape and violence were part of the daily fare of prison life.[48]

This problem is exacerbated by the existence of so-called reality television programs depicting prisons. The viewing public is largely unaware of the production processes of such media and are largely unable to determine which elements are fictitious and which are based in reality.[49] In their review of reality television programs that feature crime and prisons, Fishman and Cavender determined that such programs "blur the line between news and entertainment; some even blur the line between fact and fiction."[50]

The dubious authenticity of prison media as stems from "the artificiality of the medium, the constraints of the genre, processes of formal and informal censorship and regulation, commercial pressures and popular tastes and demand."[51] Cecil noted an additional category, the need of production companies to please the prison administrators in order to permit continued access.[52] Historically, prison officials are typically reticent to allow media access.[53] Therefore, should the message produced by the media conflict with the needs and desires, officials can and will prohibit further filming within their institutions. Further, production companies face a public unwilling to allow a counter-narrative of prisoners as anything other than reprobate. Attempting to use media to humanize prisoners is "taken as a sign of indifference to the suffering of those who have been harmed by others and of lack of common sense in the face of obvious social dangers."[54] Under the pressures noted above, "the editing process results in countless hours of film on the cutting-room floor, thus creating a highly edited version of prison life."[55]

Made-for-TV and made-for-film prisons, however, are far different from their real counterparts. Yousman critiqued television programs for portraying prison as far more violent than reality and for failing to address salient issues to carceral life. He interviewed former prisoners about their impressions of fictional prison media and they generally rejected the fictional portrayals' accuracy:

> Interviewees also spontaneously brought up many issues that were rarely or never dealt with in either dramatic or news programming. Issues such as poor nutritional and health care services; limited opportunities to participate in educational, vocational, or other rehabilitation programs; frequent verbal or physical abuse by corrections staff; complicity of corrections staff with the prison drug trade; the difficulties released prisoners have in finding employment; and high turnover rates and inadequate training programs for COs, came up in every interview and yet were almost entirely absent from the television discourse about incarceration.[56]

Despite these inaccuracies, prison media continues to shape the public's perceptions of life behind bars, leading viewers to believe about prisoners the same things the show's creators want them to believe about fictional characters.

A primary reason for the limited scope and unified message about prisoners stems from the limitations imposed by the carceral system on inmate communication. While the past decades have seen a rise in access to electronic and print media inside prison walls, the modes of communication available to prisoners are almost invariably one-way, from the outside in. Vickery wrote about the digital divide that results from economic inequality.[57] According to their study, numerous individuals lack meaningful access to communication technology like cellular phones and home computers due to the economic constraints of their impoverished financial class. Prisoners, however, are not prohibited from possessing telecommunication devices because they cannot afford them, but by policy. Texas, like many other states, prohibits and heavily punishes prisoners for possession of cellphones. Further, in most states, prisoners are either prohibited entirely from accessing the internet or are limited only to secure servers displaying only approved material for educational and job seeking purposes.

In their analysis of media restrictions imposed on youth, Vickery argued that prohibition of access to content stems a risk-aversion model where adults see technology as a threat to youth.[58] The prison system, on the other hand, sees prisoners, rather than technology, as the threat to be contained. Jewkes and Reisdorf, in one of only a handful of articles examining prisoner media access, confirmed through their study that fear and risk-aversion are the foundation for media-prohibitive policies in prison, writing:

> The biggest fears surrounded online media, but even technologies that are not internet- enabled, but could potentially be converted, were vetoed by security officers because, as one of them put it, 'you'll always find some bright spark who can take an iPod or games console and convert it to watch pornography or contact people outside that they shouldn't'. This is a deeply entrenched and oft-repeated view, which underlines current rationales for punishment and belies an overt risk-aversion.[59]

Prison officials worry that "the introduction and spread of digital infrastructures on the grounds that they carry risks of inappropriate networking, prisoner organization, resistance, mobilization and access to 'risky' content"[60] While Vickery argued that we ought to abandon risk-aversion models of media access in favor of policies that are opportunity-driven, the adoption of this mindset is unlikely within a prison environment. So long as prisons view inmates as threats in need of correction, access to the internet and other means of outside communication conflict "with commonplace ideas about incarceration being a time of isolation, solitude and penitence, as well as retribution, material hardship and suffering."[61] As such, there remains primarily only one narrative circulating about prisoners.

Fear Sells

Within these conditions, the public accepts the fictional and quasi-fictional representations of prison through this media as accurate and uses these beliefs to shape their actions and reactions. As such, the "portrayal of crime and justice in the media has been forwarded as also influencing the public agenda for justice by sensitizing the public to particular issues."[62] Munro-Bjorklund expanded on this argument, stating that "public attitudes toward criminals in general, the types of people who are or should be incarcerated, and prison conditions that should be tolerated become evident through the treatment of criminal characters in film"[63] Finally, Mathiesen claimed that "in the whole range of media, the prison is simply not recognised as a fiasco, but as a necessary if not always fully successful method of reaching its purported goals"[64] This type of media exposure "can leave the recipient of such information feeling that they are appropriately informed about the reality of the prison, and with little or no desire to challenge such evidence."[65]

The problems of public perceptions do not stop simply by shaping the views of media consumers. In a representative democracy like the United States, mass opinions bleed into public policies. "As a consequence, such distorted media discourses profoundly influence not only public attitudes, but also political rhetoric and subsequently criminal justice policies."[66] The "War on Drugs," a reaction to public perceptions of a rising crime rate in relation to illicit drug use despite no empirical evidence, is a prime example of these effects.[67] Despite being based in fictive ideas, the War on Drugs led to a significant increase in incarceration rates, particularly among minorities.[68] According to Rapping, media consumers are:

> determined to keep themselves safe in what they perceived as a social landscape filled with mass murderers run amok, with teenage 'superpredators,' and with murder and mayhem around every corner. In reality, statistics show a dramatically declining crime rate.[69]

This fear, an effect of media consumption, "is used to support public policies, or more conservatively, this fear is needed to maintain an active public indifference or ignorance around the establishment of regressive and punitive policies and laws."[70] This fear forms the basis for convictism.

Notes

1 Peyton Reed, "Ant-Man" (Marvel Studios, 2015).
2 Adam Key and Natalie Craig, "Audience Analysis," in *International Public Debate Association Textbook*, ed. Patrick G Richey and Katelyn E Brooks (New York: Kendall Hunt, 2020).

3 U.S. Congress, House Of Representatives-Wednesday, April 20, 1994 H2628 (Congressional Record 1994).
4 This section is adapted from Adam Key, "In the first degree: A study of effective discourse in postsecondary prison education" (Ph.D. Dissertation, Texas A&M University, 2018).
5 Erving Goffman, *Asylums: Essays on the social situation of mental patients and other inmates* (Boston, MA: AldineTransaction, 1961).
6 Louise Ridley, "No substitute for the real thing: The impact of prison-based work experience on students' thinking about imprisonment," *The Howard Journal of Crime and Justice* 53, no. 1 (2014): 17.
7 David B Wilson, "Lights, camera, action," *Prison Report* 60, no. 1 (2003): 28.
8 Ray Surette, *Media, crime and criminal justice: Images, realities and policies* (Belmont, CA: Wadsworth Publishing Company, 2007).
9 Jeremy H Lipschultz and Michael L Hilt, *Crime and local television news: Dramatic, breaking, and live from the scene* (London: Routledge, 2014).
10 Surette, *Media, crime and criminal justice*, 1.
11 Marie Gillespie et al., *Media and the shaping of public knowledge and attitudes towards crime and punishment*, Rethinking Crime & Punishment (London: University of London Press, 2003).
12 Ray Surette, "Performance crime and justice," *Current Issues in Criminal Justice* 27 (2015): 195–216.
13 Ray Surette, "Some unpopular thoughts about popular culture," in *Popular culture, crime, and justice*, ed Frankie Y. Bailey and Donna C. Hale (Belmont, CA: West/Wadsworth, 1998): xiv–xxiv.
14 Frankie Y Bailey and Donna C Hale, *Popular culture, crime, and justice* (Belmont, CA: West/Wadsworth, 1998).
15 Douglas Snauffer, *Crime television* (Westport, CT: Greenwood Publishing Group, 2006).
16 Surette, *Media, crime and criminal justice*.
17 Dawn K Cecil, *Prison life in popular culture: From the big house to orange is the new black* (Boulder, CO: Lynne Rienner Publishers, 2015).
18 Sean O'Sullivan, "Representations of prison in nineties Hollywood cinema: from Con Air to The Shawshank Redemption," *The Howard Journal of Crime and Justice* 40, no. 4 (2001): 317–34.
19 Leonidas K Cheliotis, "The ambivalent consequences of visibility: Crime and prisons in the mass media," *Crime, Media, Culture* 6, no. 2 (2010): 175.
20 Elayne Rapping, *Law and justice as seen on TV* (New York: NYU Press, 2003), 81.
21 Mike Nellis, "Future punishment in American science fiction films," in *Captured by the media*, ed. P Mason (Cullompton: Willan, 2013), 223.
22 Nicole Hahn Rafter, *Shots in the mirror: Crime films and society* (Oxford: Oxford University Press, 2006), 164.
23 Wilson, "Lights, camera, action," 79.
24 O'Sullivan, "Representations of prison in nineties Hollywood cinema," 321.
25 Austin Sarat, *When the state kills: Capital punishment and the American condition* (Princeton, NJ: Princeton University Press, 2002), 82.
26 Michel Foucault, *Discipline and punish: The birth of the prison* (New York: Vintage, 1977), 10.

27 Foucault, *Discipline and punish*, 10.
28 Dario Llinares, "Punishing bodies: British prison film and the spectacle of masculinity," *Journal of British Cinema and Television* 12, no. 2 (2015): 210.
29 Paul Mason, "Relocating Hollywood's prison film discourse," in *Captured by the media*, ed. P Mason (Cullompton: Willan Publishing, 2005), 195.
30 Surette, "Some unpopular thoughts about popular culture."
31 Paul Mason, "The screen machine: Cinematic representations of prison," in *Criminal visions: Media representations of crime and justice*, ed. P Mason (Cullompton: Willan Publishing, 2003): 278–97.
32 Cheliotis, "The ambivalent consequences of visibility: Crime and prisons in the mass media," 178.
33 Llinares, "Punishing bodies," 211.
34 Edward Herman and Noam Chomsky, *Manufacturing consent: The political economy of the mass media* (New York: Pantheon, 1990).
35 Derral Cheatwood, "Films about adult, male, civilian prisons," in *Popular culture, crime and justice*, ed. Frankie Y Bailey and Donna C Hale (New York: Wadsworth, 1998): 209–31.
36 David L Altheide, "The news media, the problem frame, and the production of fear," *The Sociological Quarterly* 38, no. 4 (1997): 651.
37 Gaye Tuchman, *Making news: A study in the construction of reality* (Belmont, CA: Thomson Wadsworth, 1978).
38 This section is adapted from Key, "In the first degree."
39 Joe R Feagin, *The white racial frame: Centuries of racial framing and counter-framing* (London: Routledge, 2010).
40 Feagin, *The white racial frame*, 141.
41 Albert Bandura and Richard H Walters, *Social learning and personality development* (New York: Holt, Rinehart, & Winston, 1963).
42 Albert Bandura, "Social-learning theory of identificatory processes," in *Handbook of socialization theory and research*, ed. DA Goslin (Chicago, IL: Rand McNally, 1969): 213–62.
43 Bandura, "Social-learning theory of identificatory processes," 215.
44 Adam Key, "A girl worth fighting for: A rhetorical critique of Disney princess Mulan's bisexuality," *Journal of Bisexuality* 15, no. 2 (2015): 268–86.
45 George Gerbner et al., "Growing up with television: Cultivation processes," *Media Effects: Advances in Theory and Research* 2 (2002): 43–67.
46 George Gerbner et al., "The "mainstreaming" of America: Violence profile," *Journal of Communication* 30, no. 3 (1980): 10–29.
47 Rafter, *Shots in the mirror: Crime films and society*.
48 Jan Van den Bulck and Heidi Vandebosch, "When the viewer goes to prison: learning fact from watching fiction. A qualitative cultivation study," *Poetics* 31, no. 2 (2003): 108.
49 Dawn K Cecil and Jennifer L Leitner, "Unlocking the gates: An examination of MSNBC Investigates–Lockup," *The Howard Journal of Crime and Justice* 48, no. 2 (2009).
50 Mark Fishman and Gray Cavender, *Entertaining crime: Television reality programs* (New York: Transaction Publishers, 1998), 3.
51 David B Wilson and Sean O'Sullivan, "Re-theorizing the penal reform functions of the prison film: Revelation, humanization, empathy and benchmarking," *Theoretical Criminology* 9, no. 4 (2005): 478.

52 Dawn K Cecil, 'Looking beyond caged heat: Media images of women in prison," *Feminist Criminology* 2, no. 4 (2007): 304–26.
53 Charles Turnbo, "News at eleven," *Federal Prisons Journal* 3 (1992): 47–51.
54 Lorna A Rhodes, *Total confinement: Madness and reason in the maximum security prison*, vol. 7 (Los Angeles: University of California Press, 2004), 6.
55 Cecil, "Looking beyond caged heat," 308.
56 Bill Yousman, *Prime time prisons on US TV: Representation of incarceration*, vol. 10 (Durham, NC: Peter Lang, 2009), 43.
57 Jacqueline Ryan Vickery, *Worried about the wrong things: Youth, risk, and opportunity in the digital world* (Cambridge: The MIT Press, 2017).
58 Vickery, *Worried about the wrong things.*
59 Yvonne Jewkes and Bianca C Reisdorf, "A brave new world: The problems and opportunities presented by new media technologies in prisons," *Criminology & Criminal Justice* 16, no. 5 (2016): 548.
60 Jewkes and Reisdorf, "A brave new world," 549.
61 Jewkes and Reisdorf, "A brave new world," 537.
62 Ray Surette, *Justice and the media: Issues and research* (Springfield, IL: C. C. Thomas, 1984), 5.
63 Vicky Munro-Bjorklund, "Popular cultural images of criminals and prisoners since Attica," *Social justice* 18, no. 3 (1991): 56–57.
64 Thomas Mathiesen, "Driving forces behind prison growth: The mass media," *Nordisk Tidsskrift for Kriminalvidenskab* 83, no. 2 (1995): 144.
65 Ridley, "No substitute for the real thing," 18.
66 Ridley, "No substitute for the real thing," 20.
67 James Austin and John Irwin, *It's about time: America's imprisonment binge* (Boston, MA: Cengage Learning, 2012).
68 Michael Lynch, *Big prisons, big dreams: Crime and the failure of America's penal system* (New Brunswick, NJ: Rutgers University Press, 2007).
69 Rapping, *Law and justice as seen on TV*, 73.
70 Erica R Meiners, "Life after Oz: Ignorance, mass media, and making public enemies," *The Review of Education, Pedagogy, and Cultural Studies* 29, no. 1 (2007): 36.

References

Altheide, David L. "The News Media, the Problem Frame, and the Production of Fear." *The Sociological Quarterly* 38, no. 4 (1997): 647–68.
Austin, James, and John Irwin. *It's about Time: America's Imprisonment Binge.* Boston, MA: Cengage Learning, 2012.
Bailey, Frankie Y, and Donna C Hale. *Popular Culture, Crime, and Justice.* Belmont, CA: West/Wadsworth, 1998.
Bandura, Albert. "Social-Learning Theory of Identificatory Processes." In *Handbook of Socialization Theory and Research*, edited by DA Goslin, 213-262. Chicago, IL: Rand McNally, 1969.
Bandura, Albert, and Richard H Walters. *Social Learning and Personality Development.* New York: Holt, Rinehart, & Winston, 1963.
Cecil, Dawn K. "Looking Beyond Caged Heat: Media Images of Women in Prison." *Feminist Criminology* 2, no. 4 (2007): 304–26.

———. *Prison Life in Popular Culture: From the Big House to Orange Is the New Black*. Boulder, CO: Lynne Rienner Publishers, 2015.

Cecil, Dawn K, and Jennifer L Leitner. "Unlocking the Gates: An Examination of Msnbc Investigates–Lockup." *The Howard Journal of Crime and Justice* 48, no. 2 (2009): 184–99.

Cheatwood, Derral. "Films about Adult, Male, Civilian Prisons." In *Popular Culture, Crime and Justice*, edited by Frankie Y Bailey and Donna C Hale, 209–31. New York: Wadsworth, 1998.

Cheliotis, Leonidas K. "The Ambivalent Consequences of Visibility: Crime and Prisons in the Mass Media." *Crime, Media, Culture* 6, no. 2 (2010): 169–84.

Feagin, Joe R. *The White Racial Frame: Centuries of Racial Framing and Counter-Framing*. London: Routledge, 2010.

Fishman, Mark, and Gray Cavender. *Entertaining Crime: Television Reality Programs*. New York: Transaction Publishers, 1998.

Foucault, Michel. *Discipline and Punish: The Birth of the Prison*. New York: Vintage, 1977.

Gerbner, George, Larry Gross, Michael Morgan, and Nancy Signorielli. "The "Mainstreaming" of America: Violence Profile." *Journal of Communication* 30, no. 3 (1980): 10–29.

Gerbner, George, Larry Gross, Michael Morgan, Nancy Signorielli, and James Shanahan. "Growing up with Television: Cultivation Processes." *Media Effects: Advances in Theory and Research* 2 (2002): 43–67.

Gillespie, Marie, Eugene McLaughlin, Stephanie Adams, and Anthea Symmonds. *Media and the Shaping of Public Knowledge and Attitudes towards Crime and Punishment*. Rethinking Crime & Punishment. London: University of London Press, 2003.

Goffman, Erving. *Asylums: Essays on the Social Situation of Mental Patients and Other Inmates*. Boston, MA: AldineTransaction, 1961.

Herman, Edward, and Noam Chomsky. *Manufacturing Consent: The Political Economy of the Mass Media*. New York: Pantheon, 1990.

Jewkes, Yvonne, and Bianca C Reisdorf. "A Brave New World: The Problems and Opportunities Presented by New Media Technologies in Prisons." *Criminology & Criminal Justice* 16, no. 5 (2016): 534–51.

Key, Adam. "A Girl Worth Fighting For: A Rhetorical Critique of Disney Princess Mulan's Bisexuality." *Journal of Bisexuality* 15, no. 2 (2015): 268–86.

———. "In the First Degree: A Study of Effective Discourse in Postsecondary Prison Education." Ph.D. Dissertation, Texas A&M University, 2018.

Key, Adam, and Natalie Craig. "Audience Analysis." In *International Public Debate Association Textbook*, edited by Patrick G Richey and Katelyn E Brooks, 96–108. New York: Kendall Hunt, 2020.

Lipschultz, Jeremy H, and Michael L Hilt. *Crime and Local Television News: Dramatic, Breaking, and Live from the Scene*. London: Routledge, 2014.

Llinares, Dario. "Punishing Bodies: British Prison Film and the Spectacle of Masculinity." *Journal of British Cinema and Television* 12, no. 2 (2015): 207–28.

54 *Shawshank Irredeemable*

Lynch, Michael. *Big Prisons, Big Dreams: Crime and the Failure of America's Penal System.* New Brunswick, NJ: Rutgers University Press, 2007.

Mason, Paul. "Relocating Hollywood's Prison Film Discourse." In *Captured by the Media,* edited by P Mason, 191–209. Cullompton: Willan Publishing, 2005.

———. "The Screen Machine: Cinematic Representations of Prison." In *Criminal Visions: Media Representations of Crime and Justice,* edited by P Mason, 278–97. Cullompton: Willan Publishing, 2003.

Mathiesen, Thomas. "Driving Forces Behind Prison Growth: The Mass Media." *Nordisk Tidsskrift for Kriminalvidenskab* 83, no. 2 (1995): 133–43.

Meiners, Erica R. "Life after Oz: Ignorance, Mass Media, and Making Public Enemies." *The Review of Education, Pedagogy, and Cultural Studies* 29, no. 1 (2007): 23–63.

Munro-Bjorklund, Vicky. "Popular Cultural Images of Criminals and Prisoners since Attica." *Social Justice* 18, no. 3 (1991): 48–70.

Nellis, Mike. "Future Punishment in American Science Fiction Films." In *Captured by the Media,* edited by P Mason, 210–28. Cullompton: Willan, 2013.

O'Sullivan, Sean. "Representations of Prison in Nineties Hollywood Cinema: From Con Air to the Shawshank Redemption." *The Howard Journal of Crime and Justice* 40, no. 4 (2001): 317–34.

Rafter, Nicole Hahn. *Shots in the Mirror: Crime Films and Society.* Oxford: Oxford University Press, 2006.

Rapping, Elayne. *Law and Justice as Seen on Tv.* New York: NYU Press, 2003.

Reed, Peyton. "Ant-Man." Marvel Studios, 2015.

Rhodes, Lorna A. *Total Confinement: Madness and Reason in the Maximum Security Prison,* vol. 7. Los Angeles: University of California Press, 2004.

Ridley, Louise. "No Substitute for the Real Thing: The Impact of Prison-Based Work Experience on Students' Thinking about Imprisonment." *The Howard Journal of Crime and Justice* 53, no. 1 (2014): 16–30.

Sarat, Austin. *When the State Kills: Capital Punishment and the American Condition.* Princeton, NJ: Princeton University Press, 2002.

Snauffer, Douglas. *Crime Television.* Westport, CT: Greenwood Publishing Group, 2006.

Surette, Ray. *Justice and the Media: Issues and Research,* Springfield, IL: C. C. Thomas, 1984.

———. *Media, Crime and Criminal Justice: Images, Realities and Policies.* Belmont, CA: Wadsworth Publishing Company, 2007.

———. "Performance Crime and Justice." *Current Issues in Criminal Justice* 27 (2015): 195-216.

———. "Some Unpopular Thoughts about Popular Culture." *Popular Culture, Crime, and Justice,* edited by Frankie Y. Bailey and Donna C. Hale, xiv-xxiv. Belmont, CA: West/Wadsworth. 1998.

Tuchman, Gaye. *Making News: A Study in the Construction of Reality.* Belmont, CA: Thomson Wadsworth, 1978.

Turnbo, Charles. "News at Eleven." *Federal Prisons Journal* 3 (1992): 47-51.

U.S. Congress. *House of Representatives-Wednesday, April 20, 1994* Congressional Record, 1994.

Van den Bulck, Jan, and Heidi Vandebosch. "When the Viewer Goes to Prison: Learning Fact from Watching Fiction. A Qualitative Cultivation Study." *Poetics* 31, no. 2 (2003): 103–16.

Vickery, Jacqueline Ryan. *Worried about the Wrong Things: Youth, Risk, and Opportunity in the Digital World.* Cambridge: The MIT Press, 2017.

Wilson, David B. "Lights, Camera, Action." *Prison Report* 60, no. 1 (2003): 27–29.

Wilson, David B, and Sean O'Sullivan. "Re-Theorizing the Penal Reform Functions of the Prison Film: Revelation, Humanization, Empathy and Benchmarking." *Theoretical Criminology* 9, no. 4 (2005): 471–91.

Yousman, Bill. *Prime Time Prisons on Us Tv: Representation of Incarceration*, vol. 10, Durham, NC: Peter Lang, 2009.

4 Convictism

While distinctive in itself, the American criminal justice system owes an extraordinary part of its establishment to the country's past as part of the British Empire. Our common law system itself, practiced in the federal judiciary and every state except Louisiana, is an offshoot of their justice system. Colin Dayan gave a detailed history of the English criminal justice tradition of civil and social death.[1] An individual sentenced for an unlawful offense got three essential disciplines: they relinquished their assets to the state, they forfeited their civil rights, and their blood was considered spoiled. Notwithstanding their middle age starting point and America's claim that it has progressed beyond the Dark Ages, every one of the three disciplines are still, in actuality, in some structure today. Rather than labeling the practice relinquishment of property to the crown, we now have laws that permit the state to hold onto property supposedly acquired by unlawful methods. The United States also denies convicts their civil liberties. Indeed, even after release, men and women are unable to exercise their Second Amendment right to bear arms nationwide and to cast a ballot for elected office in most jurisdictions. The final punishment, the doctrine of corruption of blood, is the most salient to this discussion. We no longer treat the physical blood itself as the source of criminal behavior, much in the same way we no longer continue the practices of 18th- and 19th-century doctors who treated diseases with bloodletting and leeches. Instead, the nation has decided that another part of the criminal is corrupt: their mind.[2]

The previous chapters overviewed the process of the development of the American public's negative attitudes toward prisoners and criminals. Understanding how the process happens, however, does not answer why it happens. That is, what is it about the media that makes the viewing public so ready to accept its claims of prisoners' lacking morality as reality? What is it about politicians that make them so

DOI: 10.4324/9781003189947-4

eager to score points by passing laws that hurt criminals but raise the crime rate? What is it about the public that makes them hate criminals more than they hate crime? The answer to that question lies within the rhetoric of convictism.

What Is Convictism?

Convictism is the belief that those without criminal convictions are wholly superior – intellectually, morally, and socially – to those with criminal convictions. It follows the same patterns of racism, sexism, homophobia, and all other forms of institutional bigotry and systemic discrimination. It is rooted in a rhetorical positioning of us vs. them, where we are the deserving heroes and they the unworthy villains. Since we have not been convicted of a crime, we believe that anyone who has possesses a reprobate mind and a criminal personality.[3] After all, we've all been tempted to break the law on occasion, but we resisted the urge, so why can't they? The answer must be because we are morally superior to them, not that their choices fundamentally differed from our own. Much like white people refuse to see their own privilege as the reason they experience more financial success than people of color, Americans fail to acknowledge systems which allow their success within the bounds of the law while denying the same abilities and opportunities to others. As such, the same mentality that blames Black people failing on a "ghetto" mentality and believes women are not suited for leadership roles because they are too "emotional" is the same discriminatory force which leads the so-called law-abiding citizen to believe that prisoners are incarcerated because they "chose" to break the law.

The existence and invisibility of convictism is perhaps best explained through Social Dominance Theory.[4] Taking an interdisciplinary approach, Sidanius and Pratto explained that social hierarchies, the foundation for systemic biases, form as societies began to acquire wealth and resources. This material and symbolic capital, which are limited resources, are hoarded by certain groups while others are given the bare minimum. Ingroups who had access to this stockpile of capital became endowed with high levels of positive social value, while outgroups with little access were stricken with extreme measures of negative social value. As such, the dominant rhetoric becomes that those with positive social value are deserving of their wealth, while those with negative social value are not. A modern example of this is the Trump tax cut bill for the ultra-wealthy. This partisan action was hailed as a victory by conservatives who hold CEOs up as "job creators," conveniently ignoring that the working- and middle-class customers are the actual source of the creation of new employment.[5] Simultaneously, those same conservatives in the Senate refused to grant those same American workers, who had negative social value, more than a $600 stimulus check in late 2020. Senate Majority Leader Mitch McConnell, Republican of Kentucky, said his fellow party members believed that "we've already done enough" financial assistance for them.[6] The rich were entitled to receive millions in funds from Congress, but the poor should be grateful for the few hundred dollars it saw fit to gift them.

Consistent with Social Dominance Theory, "prejudice, racism, stereotypes and discrimination simply cannot be understood outside the conceptual framework of group-based social hierarchy, especially within social systems of economic surplus."[7] These social hierarches, however, are neither naturally occurring, nor self-maintaining. To perpetuate these systems, their inherent nature must be subscribed to both by the oppressors and, more importantly, the oppressed. The primary tool used to create and maintain systems of social dominance is rhetoric which "influences popular attitudes and beliefs, even to the extent of molding the core taken-for-granted assumptions that guide and constrain our actions and interpretations of reality."[8] This rhetoric takes place in a multiplicity of forms including language, myth, and rituals.

The Language of Criminality

The English language currently lacks a broad umbrella term to encompass both prisoners/criminals and non-prisoners/criminals in the way that terms like Race, Religion, Sex, Gender, and Sexual Orientation include members of various groups within them. The terms "prisoner" and "criminal" meet the definition of "what rhetorical scholar Michael McGee describes as an "ideograph": a shorthand word or phrase that captures and organizes community around prevailing ideological commitments."[9] To society at large, a person labeled as a 'criminal' or 'prisoner' is a savage worthy of mistreatment. At the so-called "Mother of All Rallies," a sparsely attended rally in favor of Donald Trump held in Washington, D.C. in September 2017, the organizers took the unusual step of allowing the leader of the Black Lives Matter protest to give a short speech on stage. When the BLM speaker referenced Eric Garner by complaining that there was no justice for a Black man that was choked to death by police officers on video, the crowd booed and one attendee could be heard loudly remarking, "He was a criminal! No! He was a criminal!" In the eyes of that attendee, being a criminal justified being killed without trial. Those labeled with the ideograph "criminal," then are seen as worthy of mistreatment, beatings, and even death by members of the American public.

Merriam-Webster's Thesaurus has a small list of antonyms for "prisoner" as well as the noun usage of "criminal" which all describe various positions related to being a prison guard or warden. When searching the term "criminal" as an adjective, the antonyms are mostly moral claims including ethical, good, just, principled, right, righteous, and virtuous. Embedded within our language, then, is both a clear us vs. them distinction as well as claims toward the immorality of prisoners and criminals. Further, there is no term to describe a person who has a bias against criminals and prisoners. That is, there is no equivalent to racism, sexism, or homophobia to describe a system of bias against criminals and prisoners.

The Myth of Neoliberalism

Beyond language, a reason that the public so easily accepts the immoral caricatures of criminals and prisoners in media along with discrimination against them – what other group would they tolerate denying the right to vote or earn gainful employment? – in public policy is the nation's belief in the myth of neoliberalism. Melamed explained that neoliberalism arose as a new form of justification for discriminatory action following World War II, a type of cultural racism that replaced its biological predecessor.[10] Unlike past forms of institutional bias, neoliberalism avoids blatantly discriminating against people on the basis of a categorical difference like race. Instead, it offers a cultural fiction that systemic discrimination does not exist and that those who fail to live up to societal standards "based on their adherence to normative cultural criteria, that is, the heterosexual family unit, middle-class status, and patriotism" do so because of their personal failures.[11] The adoption of neoliberalism proffered a uniform "U.S. national culture as the key to achieving America's manifest destiny and proof of American exceptionalism."[12]

Under the neoliberal paradigm, the so-called free market is the solution to ending inequality. By ignoring existing system barriers as if they no longer exist, neoliberalism promotes a fictional nation where everyone is on an equal playing field and has the same chance at success or failure based on individual choices. By denying systemic inequality, the public remains comfortable in its "beliefs that laziness and weak will are the chief impediments to [criminals' and prisoners'] social mobility."[13] After all, they experienced hardships in their own lives and never turned to committing crimes, so why couldn't criminals and prisoners have simply worked harder instead of breaking the law?

Orange Is The New Black offers powerful evidence for neoliberalism's presence within prison media, ironically in the beginning of the pilot episode. Piper, the main character, is in a conversation with her mother who insists that she does not belong in prison with the rest of the inmates. Piper immediately rebuffs her mother "by reminding viewers that being incarcerated is 'nobody's fault but [her] own.'"[14] This emphasis on personal choice being the sole determinant for consequences is a foundational tenet of neoliberalism. In a statement that is meant to rebuff her mother's claims of privilege and establish solidarity with her fellow inmates, largely people of color, Piper's statement enforces neoliberal ideas in a "complicitous critique" which is inherently "bound up... with its own complicity with power and domination."[15]

Neoliberalism, therefore, exists as a hidden discourse permeating prison media. Belief in the neoliberal ideology, embedded in American culture, means that narratives of prisoners are more easily accepted. Returning to Cultivation theory, the American public mostly experiences substitution in regard to information about prisons, but the neoliberal messages cause resonance with their taken-for-granted beliefs about choice.

The Ritual of Punishment

Punishment, as defined by Durkheim, is a societal response to violating the collective consciousness which he defined as the "totality of beliefs and sentiments common to the average member of a society [which] forms a determinate system with a life of its own."[16] The problem with this, of course, is that those common ideas are themselves rhetorical creations from the same system perpetuating the hierarchies which create and maintain social dominance. As such, those in power both create the rules which supply the collective consciousness with ideals and engage in elaborate punishments for those who threaten their self-declared power by violating them.

When a person violates the law, they are faced with a penal ritual like arrest, trial, and imprisonment. These "penal rituals – which are, by definition, public, organized and fervent – express and solidify the sacred values of a given society, while drawing symbolic boundaries between in-groups and out-groups."[17] In practice, it works like this:

first, a member of society allegedly commits a crime; second, they are arrested by police officers and forced to stand trial where a jury of their supposed peers finds them guilty and a judge sentences them to prison; finally, they are incarcerated by the state for a set number of days or years, effectively and literally removed from society. Of particular note within this ritual are the costumes worn by the various players. Hearkening back to medieval kingdoms, police officers wear a uniform representing the state emblazoned with a metal shield. Judges, clad in black ceremonial robes, sit behind a bench in a seat of power purposefully constructed significantly higher than any of the rest in the courtroom and wield a gavel they clack down to signal their rulings or keep order. Attorneys wear expensive suits, a type of clothing that marks them as the high social value wealthy, where the defendant is either dressed in street clothes or a jail uniform if they cannot afford a suit themselves.

Much like college graduations, there is fundamentally no practical reason why judges still wear robes. In fact, in many judicial procedures where the only people present are attorneys and the judge, the robe will not be worn. It is strictly a performative costume used to promote the legitimacy of the ritual they engage in. While an American might laugh at the idea that British courts still use powdered wigs as something of a comical historic relic, judges wear robes and police officer wear badges in the shape of shields for much the same reason. These symbolic boundaries establish the ingroup wears one uniform, where the outgroup, the prisoner, will wear an entirely different one during their incarceration.

The "War on Criminals" Declared

Joshua Page described the phenomenon of the debate over the 1994 crime bill as a scenario where "lawmakers, in concert with the popular media, produced a *legislative penal drama* – complete with heroes and villains, action and suspense and colorful imagery – in which they spoke to key audiences' (specifically, white working and middle class voters')."[18] For the conservative Democrats and Republicans purveying the drama, the obvious villains were the undeserving prisoners, while they were the heroes saving the law-abiding students allegedly being denied Pell grants from being victimized.

Both Hutchison and Gordon contrasted the undeserving inmates receiving Pell funds with the children of police officers who were denied them. They could have easily chosen stories of the children of any number of parents whose professions put them just above the maximum cutoff line for receiving a Pell grant. They did not, however, choose to talk about children of soldiers, steelworkers, firefighters, or nurses. While some analyzing this have argued that their efforts were an attempt to attack those in poverty in the same way Reagan lambasted "welfare queens," I believe this rhetorical selection of the children of police is prime evidence that the bias they were invoking was convictist. In fact, they repeatedly made appeals to the working poor, noting "Pell grants were created to help low and middle-income students get the education they need to improve their lives."[19] It was not an opposition to those in poverty, but those in poverty for the wrong reasons. As such, this choice was strategic to inflame convictist biases. After all, who is a better foil to a lawbreaker than the child of someone sworn to uphold the law? No one illustrated this more succinctly than Gordon who said "law-abiding students have every right to be outraged when a Pell grant for a policeman's child is cut but a criminal that the officer sends to prison can still get a big check."[20] In this mythical scenario, the hard-working child of a police officer is valued less by society than the criminals their parent put away.

Furthermore, the legislators repeatedly tried to drive a rhetorical wedge between incarcerated and non-incarcerated students. Fields, in his statement, refers to inmates as not only prisoners, but "incarcerated prisoners" on four separate occasions in his roughly one-minute rant. He contrasted this with the "students" who were "son[s] and daughters" as if prisoners receiving Pell weren't college students and didn't have parents.[21] This was not the first time they would make this distinction. In the 1992 debate attempting to remove Pell eligibility from prisoners, Gordon argued

> Let me remind Members that every time that a prisoner gets a Pell grant that means a traditional student does not get a Pell grant. Not only do they not get it, but since prisoners have no income, they are first in line. So nobody else gets a Pell grant until all of the prisoners, with no income, get what they want.[22]

Despite the claim of any eligible student being denied a Pell grant being an obvious fabrication, this argument also serves to further the rhetorical divide between "traditional students" and prisoners. Additionally, this conveniently ignores the fact that the Pell grant is based on expected family contribution (EFC), which is calculated by income. Even if his argument about being "first in line" were somehow true, prisoners with no income would be at the exact same place in line with anyone whose parents made so little that their EFC was zero.

However, even those defending prisoners' ability to get Pell grants were not immune from convictism. Senator Pell, for instance, attacked Hutchison for her amendment removing eligibility from the federal financial aid program bearing his name by quoting an editorial from the *Washington Post* which concluded by saying

> As Congress finishes work on what is expected to be a $22 billion crime bill, no increased funding for education programs is in the legislation. It's the other way. The Senate backed an amendment--sponsored by Kay Bailey Hutchison (R-Texas), who is currently under felony indictment for political abuses--to deny prisoners college courses under Pell grants.[23]

Both the author of the editorial and Senator Pell rhetorically argued that Hutchison was inferior because she was indicted for a felony. While it might be argued that Pell was trying to use this article to establish a level of hypocrisy in that Hutchison, a potential felon herself, authored an amendment denying other felons federal assistance, the intent is immaterial to the effect. Even under that scenario, Pell's essential argument was that the Senate ought not listen to what Hutchison had to say because she was potentially a convict. As such, he appealed to their convictist beliefs that they, being apparently law-abiding, were superior to Hutchison.

While the transformation had been building for some time, the revocation of Pell grant eligibility for prisoners in 1994 is the moment where the "War on Crime" ended and the "War on Criminals" began. It did not matter that postsecondary education programs inside prison walls rapidly reduced recidivism. The legislators who voted for this bill did not care that they would be saving countless people from becoming victims of crime in the future. The goal, at this point, ceased to be preventing crime and became instead hurting criminals.

More Than Stigma

On its face, one might assume convictism is simply the stigma of incarceration or criminality. Upon closer examination, however, it is clear that convictism is something else entirely. Stigma is certainly part of it – just as it is part of racism, sexism, homophobia, and other forms of systemic bias and discrimination – but it does not constitute the whole. As will be made clear below, prisoners suffer from stigma, but they also suffer from convictism.

What Is Stigma?

The modern study of stigma began with Erving Goffman in his seminal text, *Stigma: Notes on the Management of a Spoiled Identity*.[24] The term itself goes back to ancient Greece where prisoners, criminals, insurrectionists, and enslaved people would have marks burned or cut into their skin to mark them as an undesirable underclass. While society no longer physically marks stigmatized people, they do so rhetorically. According to Goffman:

> While the stranger is present before us, evidence can arise of his possessing an attribute that makes him different from others in the category of persons available for him to be, and of a less desirable kind in the extreme, a person who is quite thoroughly bad, or dangerous, or weak. He is thus reduced in our minds from a whole and usual person to a tainted, discounted one. Such an attribute is a stigma, especially when its discrediting effect is very extensive; sometimes it is also called a failing, a shortcoming, a handicap.[25]

Goffman presented three primary types of stigma: physical deformity, deviation in personal characteristics, and tribal stigma. The stigma of physical deformity stems from the perceptions of those physically different than others, like someone in a wheelchair or a person with Down syndrome. The stigma of deviation in personal characteristics covers a wider variety of what society would view as character flaws, "being perceived as weak willed, domineering, rigid in one's beliefs, or dishonest, for example."[26] Finally, tribal stigma involves being a member of a stigmatized group like race, sex, or religion.

While much has been written about stigma since Goffman, most scholars on the topic are in agreement that there are two necessary elements of the phenomenon. First, the difference of a stigmatized person from societal norms must be both recognized and devalued.[27] Second, stigma only occurs within social interaction.[28] A person is not stigmatized within themselves, but only through their interactions with others. More than that, a stigmatized person is not stigmatized in every situation. Stigma "conveys a social identity that is devalued in a particular social context," meaning that there are contexts where a person's appearance, behavior, and group memberships are not stigmatized.[29]

John Pryor and Glenn Reeder, in discussing the stigma related to HIV, created a model that included four different dimensions of stigma: public, self, association, and institutional. At the center of their model is public stigma, which is the psychological, social, emotional, and physical reaction of others to a stigmatized person. For example, if someone feels anger or fear at learning their new neighbor is a member of a stigmatized group and avoids contact with them, that is public stigma. Self-stigma is the effect of being stigmatized on the person. This includes both apprehension of public stigma as well as internalizing societal standards and viewing themselves as deviant. For instance, a gay person in a homophobic community might stay in the closet to avoid public stigma and view themselves as sexually deviant because that's the message they heard from the pulpit. Stigma by association is where the friends and family suffer similar treatment for their relationship with the stigmatized person. This occurs in scenarios like the parents of an unruly child being actively avoided by other parents in a neighborhood. Finally, structural stigmas perpetuate public stigma through institutional means. An example of this are laws which prohibit trans men and women from using public restrooms for their gender, instead forcing them into ones for their sex wrongfully assigned at birth.

Differences between Stigma and Systemic Discrimination

While stigma is certainly part of systemic discrimination, the two concepts are not synonymous. For instance, while "racial designations have become stigmatised and used in order to disempower and oppress people," racism is fundamentally different from racial stigma.[30] Even as an area of academic study, prejudice and stigma comprise distinct, yet overlapping, research areas. Studies of prejudice deal with oppression, domination, and exploitation of a subordinate group by a dominant group, while stigma research deals with how society enforces normative standards.[31] All systemic discrimination involves stigma, but not all stigma involves systemic discrimination.

Take race, for example. Within the white supremacist institutional culture of the United States, being Black certainly meets Goffman's standards of stigma. Having Black skin makes a person observably different from the white norm, cultural practices like the use of African American Vernacular English (AAVE) are looked down upon as character flaws by many white employers and teachers, and being a member of a race different from the white norm is the definition of Goffman's tribal stigma. Black people face public stigma such as white flight, where white people move away en masse when too many Black people move into their neighborhoods.[32] Many Black people self-stigmatize, adopting white standards which vilify their cultural norms and replacing their manner of speaking with one more acceptable to white ears.[33] White people in interracial romantic relationships and marriages with Black partners experience stigma by association, with many receiving anything from negative verbal and nonverbal responses to being kicked out of their homes by parents who refuse to accept the relationship.[34] Finally, Black people suffer repeated structural stigmas including hiring managers who are biased against candidates with traditionally Black names.[35] Being Black is certainly stigmatized within the United States, but stigma is not the reason that George Floyd, Breonna Taylor, Eric Garner, Tamir Rice, Alton Sterling, Philando Castile, and so many other Black men were murdered by police. Racism is.

Convictism Is Systemic Discrimination

Prisoners and former prisoners certainly suffer from a variety of stigmas. They might have prison tattoos and wear uniforms that mark them as a member of a stigmatized class.[36] Their (alleged) crimes are deviations of personal characteristics.[37] And being a prisoner, complete with an ID number issued by state and federal departments of corrections, subjects them to tribal stigma.[38] They face a public stigma from citizens who think they're dangerous.[39] They self-stigmatize, believing that they're worthless, will never stop being a criminal, and are deserving of mistreatment.[40] Family members of prisoners, particularly children, suffer stigmas of association.[41] And, of course, they bear the brunt of various structural stigmas which prohibit many from achieving any type of economic success inside and outside of prison walls.[42] The stigma of incarceration, however, is not the reason Candance Owens said Floyd could never be a hero or martyr nor why the Governor of Texas decided that prisoners should die of COVID-19. Convictism is.

Convictism envelops and exceeds stigma in the same way racism and other forms of systemic discrimination do. More than simply spoiling their identity, it sets the public up in a rhetorical and often material war against them. During the snowstorm that nearly blacked out the Texas power grid in February 2020, hundreds of doses of the COVID-19 vaccine had to be immediately utilized because power loss to their refrigeration units meant they would otherwise expire. As part of this, a few hundred were sent to the county jail in Houston, along with many more being sent to a university and local medical centers. When the local news affiliates reported on this, Facebook comments loudly complained that the vaccine was given to inmates instead of, in their mind, more deserving groups like grocery store clerks. Fifty years prior, the same sentiment would have likely been just as publicly expressed if a vaccine went to Black people ahead of white people. Wishing death upon a group of people is more than just stigma and it is clear that, even in the midst of an unprecedented crisis, the public still wishes death upon prisoners.

Scale of Convictual Sentiment[43]

In their book, *The Black Image in the White Mind*, Entman and Rojecki disputed the binary dichotomy between racist and non-racist individuals.[44] Instead, they proposed a Spectrum of White Racial Sentiment that better encompassed the nuances of the American public. The scale included Comity, Ambivalence, Animosity, and Racism. Those in the Comity, commonly referred to as non-racist or anti-racist, category have positive or neutral feelings toward Black people and believe that groups vary widely in traits; that discrimination is prevalent and harmful; and that white and Black people do not have conflicting group interests. On the other end of the spectrum is the Racism category whose members have intense negative emotions toward Black people; believe they are fundamentally different and lower than white people; think that Black people cannot achieve equality and discrimination against them is a necessity; and are convinced that the interests of Black groups are a threat to white people. Ambivalence is the midpoint between Comity and Racism where members oscillate between positive and negative emotions toward Black people and believe that they tend to have more negative qualities than white people, that discrimination occurs in rare and isolated incidents, and that Black interests sometimes but not always cause problems for white interests. Finally, Animosity exists between Ambivalence and Racism and its members have mostly moderate negative emotions toward Black people and believe that they mostly have negative traits, that Black people no longer experience discrimination, and that Black political movements are asking for special treatment at the expense of white people. The authors do not offer a category between Comity and Ambivalence.

Within each of these categories, Entman and Rojecki established four different dimensions related to various facets of belief. These included Negative Homogeneity, Structural Impediments, Conflicting Group Interests, and Emotional Responses. Negative Homogeneity dealt with how much people believed behavior was the result of the individual or the racial group. Structural Impediments concerned whether people believed discrimination was prevalent and, in the case of the Racist category, necessary. Conflicting Group Interests examined whether people thought racial groups political interests were aligned or mutually exclusive. Finally, Emotional Responses consider the valence and intensity of emotional feelings related to racial issues.

I have adapted Entman and Rojecki's scale to be applicable to public sentiment toward prisoners and criminals. As a first step to understand the public's attitudes toward the incarcerated, one could simply substitute the word "prisoner" or "criminal" for "Black" and "non-prisoner" or "non-criminal" for "white" in their scale. This is helpful to map attitudes which vary from those who recognize a wide variety of traits in both groups, to those who believe in some measure of difference between criminals/prisoners and themselves, to those who believe there is a distinct and unchangeable difference between themselves and criminals/prisoners. However, the scale as currently constructed is certainly missing a category. At present, there is no space between Comity and Ambivalence, so people are either anti-racist or apathetic. Paulo Freire's notion of false charity provides an excellent and previously unrecognized midpoint. In *Pedagogy of the Oppressed*, Freire wrote that "any attempt to 'soften' the power of the oppressor in deference to the weakness of the oppressed almost always manifests itself in the form of false generosity."[45] Essentially, false charity is the phenomenon where people feel positively about oppressed groups and wish to stop their subjugation not because they recognize their inherent equality, but because they believe them to be inferior and in need of saving. Freire expounded on this notion, writing:

> [I]ndeed, the attempt never goes beyond this... in order to have the continued opportunity to express their "generosity," the oppressors must perpetuate injustice as well...An unjust social order is the permanent fount of this "generosity," which is nourished by death, despair, and poverty. That is why the dispensers of false generosity become desperate at the slightest threat to its source. True generosity consists precisely in fighting to destroy the causes which nourish false charity. False charity constrains the fearful and subdued, the "rejects of life," to extend their trembling hands. True generosity lies in striving so that these hands whether of individuals or entire peoples need be extended less and less in supplication, so that more and more they become human hands which work and, working, transform the world.[46]

Table 4.1 Scale of Convictual Sentiment

	Comity	False Charity	Ambivalence	Animosity	Convictism
Negative homogeneity	Individual prisoners and non-prisoners vary widely in traits	Prisoners tend to display more negative traits than non-prisoners, but they have no control over them	Prisoners tend to display slightly more negative traits than non-prisoners	Prisoners, on the whole, possess many more negative traits than non-prisoners	Prisoners are inherently evil and possess negative traits by nature
Structural impediments	Discrimination is widely prevalent, leading to unequal opportunity and high recidivism	Discrimination is prevalent and should be stopped because prisoners are incapable of helping themselves	Discrimination may occur occasionally, but it's not a major issue	Discrimination no longer happens; any negative treatment is justice for the crimes prisoners committed	Discrimination is fundamentally necessary because prisoners are evil, and society needs to be protected from them
Conflicting group interests	The interests of prisoners and non-prisoners are the same, cooperation is fundamentally necessary for society	Non-prisoners should make decisions for prisoners because they are incapable of making good choices	Interests of prisoners occasionally conflict with non-prisoner interests and should be overruled when they conflict	Helping prisoners means hurting non-prisoners, cooperation means non-prisoners lose in a zero-sum game	Prisoner interests are in destroying society and are extremely dangerous to non-prisoners
Emotional responses	Low intensity, positive or neutral feelings	High intensity, positive feelings about saving prisoners from themselves	Moderate intensity, varies between positive and negative	Moderate intensity, largely negative toward prisoners	High intensity, extremely negative toward prisoners

The reason I chose to label it false charity, rather than false generosity, on this scale is that generosity implies a relationship between equals, where charity necessitates a power differential. A friend may be generous with their time, but you would not describe them as charitable. At the same time, when someone says something is "for charity," it's typically also accompanied by language regarding "helping the less fortunate." When I was a graduate student, I avoided talking to one secretary because they would engage in this false charity rhetoric every time I would see them. They would nearly get tears in her eyes when they talked about how noble it was that I was helping and caring for these "poor prisoners," and that things would have been different if someone else had cared for them earlier. Every time, I bit my tongue to stop myself from shouting "they're people!" back at them.

By including false charity as the fifth category, Entman and Rojecki's original scale can be adapted not just for convictual sentiment, but for racial, sexual, and any number of other categories of systemic discrimination. The scale is presented below, but I do so with the caveat that, like any measure, it is necessarily incomplete and always-already in need of revision.

This scale, like Entman and Rojecki's, can function as a useful tool in understanding the various levels and intersections of convictist bias. Convictism, like racism and sexism, operates on multiple planes of belief. As with any other systemic bias, it is unlikely that any given person will fall entirely within a particular column. Most people will tend to occupy different columns depending on the row. Given its five-point analysis, it may be useful in the future to develop a measure of convictism. Furthermore, it provides scholars the ability to map out convictist bias in order to further understand individual, political, and societal actions. For example, the speeches from Chapter 2 could be analyzed and mapped using this table. By developing a more clear picture of how convictism functions in various avenues, it can be better identified and understood.

Notes

1 Colin Dayan, *The law is a white dog: How legal rituals make and unmake persons* (Princeton, NJ: Princeton University Press, 2011).
2 This section is adapted from Adam Key, "In the first degree: A study of effective discourse in postsecondary prison education" (Ph.D. Dissertation, Texas A&M University, 2018).
3 Jamie J Fader, *Falling back: Incarceration and transitions to adulthood among urban youth* (New Brunswick, NJ: Rutgers University Press, 2013).

4 Jim Sidanius and Felicia Pratto, *Social dominance: An intergroup theory of social hierarchy and oppression* (New York: Cambridge University Press, 2001).

5 Nick Hanauer, "Beware, fellow plutocrats, the pitchforks are coming," (TED, 2014), https://www.ted.com/talks/nick_hanauer_beware_fellow_plutocrats_the_pitchforks_are_coming.

6 Judy Woodruff and Daniel Bush, "McConnell: Some republicans think 'we have already done enough' pandemic aid," *Newshour* 2020, https://www.pbs.org/newshour/show/mcconnell-some-republicans-think-we-have-already-done-enough-pandemic-aid.

7 Sidanius and Pratto, *Social dominance*, 38.

8 Charles Conrad, *Organizational rhetoric: Strategies of resistance and domination* (Malden, MA: Polity Press, 2011), 14.

9 Dana L Cloud, ""Civility" as a threat to academic freedom," *First Amendment Studies* 49, no. 1 (2015): 13.

10 Jodi Melamed, "The spirit of neoliberalism: From racial liberalism to neoliberal multiculturalism," *Social Text* 24, no. 4 (2006): 1–24.

11 Christina Belcher, "There is no such thing as a post-racial prison: Neoliberal multiculturalism and the white savior complex on orange is the new black," *Television & New Media* 17, no. 6 (2016): 493.

12 Melamed, "The spirit of neoliberalism," 7.

13 Robert M Entman and Andrew Rojecki, *The black image in the white mind: Media and race in America* (New York: Wiley, 2001), 19.

14 Belcher, "There is no such thing as a post-racial prison," 494.

15 Linda Hutcheon, *The politics of postmodernism* (London: Routledge, 1989), 4.

16 Emile Durkheim, *The division of labor in society* (Simon and Schuster, 2014), 38–39.

17 Joshua Page, "Eliminating the enemy: The import of denying prisoners access to higher education in Clinton's America," *Punishment & Society* 6, no. 4 (2004): 360.

18 Page, "Eliminating the enemy," 360.

19 U.S. Congress, House Of Representatives-Wednesday, April 20, 1994 H7948 (Congressional Record 1994).

20 U.S. Congress, Short House Of Representatives-Wednesday, April 20, 1994 H7948.

21 U.S. Congress, Short House Of Representatives-Wednesday, April 20, 1994 H7949.

22 U.S. Congress, House of Representatives-Thursday, March 26, 1992 H1893 (Congressional Record 1992).

23 U.S. Congress, Senate-Wednesday, February 9, 1994 S1275 (Congressional Record 1994).

24 Erving Goffman, *Stigma: Notes on the management of spoiled identity* (New York: Simon and Schuster, 1963).

25 Goffman, *Stigma*, 12.

26 John Flowerdew, "Scholarly writers who use English as an additional language: What can Goffman's "stigma" tell us?" *Journal of English for Academic Purposes* 7, no. 2 (2008): 79–80.

27 Todd F Heatherton, *The social psychology of stigma* (New York: Guilford Press, 2003).

28 Michelle R Hebl and John F Dovidio, "Promoting the "social" in the examination of social stigmas," *Personality and Social Psychology Review* 9, no. 2 (2005): 156–82.

29 Jennifer Crocker, Brenda Major, and Claude Steele, "Social stigma," in *The Handbook of Social Psychology*, ed. Daniel T Gilbert, Susan T Fiske, and Gardner Lindzey (Boston, MA: McGraw-Hill, 1998), 505.

30 Suman Fernando, "Stigma, racism and power," *Aotearoa Ethnic Network Journal* 1, no. 1 (2006): 24.

31 Jo C Phelan, Bruce G Link, and John F Dovidio, "Stigma and prejudice: One animal or two?" *Social Science & Medicine* 67, no. 3 (2008): 358–67.

32 Kevin M Kruse, *White flight: Atlanta and the making of modern conservatism*, vol. 89 (Princeton, NJ: Princeton University Press, 2013).

33 Jessica R Graham et al., "The mediating role of internalized racism in the relationship between racist experiences and anxiety symptoms in a Black American sample," *Cultural Diversity and Ethnic Minority Psychology* 22, no. 3 (2016): 369–76.

34 George Yancey, "Experiencing racism: Differences in the experiences of whites married to blacks and non-black racial minorities," *Journal of Comparative Family Studies* 38, no. 2 (2007): 197–213.

35 Stevie Watson, Osei Appiah, and Corliss G Thornton, "The effect of name on pre-interview impressions and occupational stereotypes: The case of black sales job applicants," *Journal of Applied Social Psychology* 41, no. 10 (2011): 2405–20.

36 Dominique Moran, "Prisoner reintegration and the stigma of prison time inscribed on the body," *Punishment & Society* 14, no. 5 (2012): 564–83.

37 Adam Dalton Reich, *Hidden truth: Young men navigating lives in and out of juvenile prison* (Los Angeles: University of California Press, 2010).

38 Adam Key and Matthew S May, "When prisoners dare to become scholars: prison education as resistance," *Review of Communication* 19, no. 1 (2019): 1–18.

39 Reich, *Hidden truth.*

40 Wing Hong Chui and Kevin Kwok-Yin Cheng, "The mark of an ex-prisoner: Perceived discrimination and self-stigma of young men after prison in Hong Kong," *Deviant Behavior* 34, no. 8 (2013): 671–84.

41 Vicky Saunders, "What does your dad do for a living? Children of prisoners and their experiences of stigma," *Children and Youth Services Review* 90 (2018): 21–7.

42 Becky Pettit, *Invisible men: Mass incarceration and the myth of black progress* (New York: Russell Sage Foundation, 2012).

43 This section is adapted from Key, "In the first degree."

44 Entman and Rojecki, *The black image in the white mind.*

45 Paulo Freire, *Pedagogy of the oppressed* (New York: Continuum, 1970), 26.

46 Freire, *Pedagogy of the oppressed*, 26–27.

References

Belcher, Christina. "There Is No Such Thing as a Post-Racial Prison: Neoliberal Multiculturalism and the White Savior Complex on Orange Is the New Black." *Television & New Media* 17, no. 6 (2016): 491–503.

Chui, Wing Hong, and Kevin Kwok-Yin Cheng. "The Mark of an Ex-Prisoner: Perceived Discrimination and Self-Stigma of Young Men after Prison in Hong Kong." *Deviant Behavior* 34, no. 8 (2013): 671–84.

Cloud, Dana L. ""Civility" as a Threat to Academic Freedom." *First Amendment Studies* 49, no. 1 (2015): 13–17.

Conrad, Charles. *Organizational Rhetoric: Strategies of Resistance and Domination.* Malden, MA: Polity Press, 2011.

Crocker, Jennifer, Brenda Major, and Claude Steele. "Social Stigma." In *The Handbook of Social Psychology*, edited by Daniel T Gilbert, Susan T Fiske, and Gardner Lindzey, 504–53. Boston, MA: McGraw-Hill, 1998.

Dayan, Colin. *The Law Is a White Dog: How Legal Rituals Make and Unmake Persons.* Princeton, NJ: Princeton University Press, 2011.

Durkheim, Emile. *The Division of Labor in Society.* New York: Simon and Schuster, 2014.

Entman, Robert M, and Andrew Rojecki. *The Black Image in the White Mind: Media and Race in America.* New York, NY: Wiley, 2001.

Fader, Jamie J. *Falling Back: Incarceration and Transitions to Adulthood among Urban Youth.* New Brunswick, NJ: Rutgers University Press, 2013.

Fernando, Suman. "Stigma, Racism and Power." *Aotearoa Ethnic Network Journal* 1, no. 1 (2006): 24–28.

Flowerdew, John. "Scholarly Writers Who Use English as an Additional Language: What Can Goffman's "Stigma" Tell Us?" *Journal of English for Academic Purposes* 7, no. 2 (2008): 77–86.

Freire, Paulo. *Pedagogy of the Oppressed.* New York: Continuum, 1970.

Goffman, Erving. *Stigma: Notes on the Management of Spoiled Identity.* New York: Simon and Schuster, 1963.

Graham, Jessica R, Lindsey M West, Jennifer Martinez, and Lizabeth Roemer. "The Mediating Role of Internalized Racism in the Relationship between Racist Experiences and Anxiety Symptoms in a Black American Sample." *Cultural Diversity and Ethnic Minority Psychology* 22, no. 3 (2016): 369–76.

Hanauer, Nick. "Beware, Fellow Plutocrats, the Pitchforks Are Coming." TED, 2014. https://www.ted.com/talks/nick_hanauer_beware_fellow_plutocrats_the_pitchforks_are_coming.

Heatherton, Todd F. *The Social Psychology of Stigma.* New York: Guilford Press, 2003.

Hebl, Michelle R, and John F Dovidio. "Promoting the "Social" in the Examination of Social Stigmas." *Personality and Social Psychology Review* 9, no. 2 (2005): 156–82.

Hutcheon, Linda. *The Politics of Postmodernism.* London: Routledge, 1989.

Key, Adam. "In the First Degree: A Study of Effective Discourse in Postsecondary Prison Education." Ph.D. Dissertation, Texas A&M University, 2018.

Key, Adam, and Matthew S May. "When Prisoners Dare to Become Scholars: Prison Education as Resistance." *Review of Communication* 19, no. 1 (2019): 1–18.

Kruse, Kevin M. *White Flight: Atlanta and the Making of Modern Conservatism*, vol. 89. Princeton, NJ: Princeton University Press, 2013.

Melamed, Jodi. "The Spirit of Neoliberalism: From Racial Liberalism to Neoliberal Multiculturalism." *Social Text* 24, no. 4 (2006): 1–24.

Moran, Dominique. "Prisoner Reintegration and the Stigma of Prison Time Inscribed on the Body." *Punishment & Society* 14, no. 5 (2012): 564–83.

Page, Joshua. "Eliminating the Enemy: The Import of Denying Prisoners Access to Higher Education in Clinton's America." *Punishment & Society* 6, no. 4 (2004): 357–78.

Pettit, Becky. *Invisible Men: Mass Incarceration and the Myth of Black Progress.* New York: Russell Sage Foundation, 2012.

Phelan, Jo C, Bruce G Link, and John F Dovidio. "Stigma and Prejudice: One Animal or Two?" *Social science & medicine* 67, no. 3 (2008): 358–67.

Reich, Adam Dalton. *Hidden Truth: Young Men Navigating Lives in and out of Juvenile Prison.* Los Angeles: University of California Press, 2010.

Saunders, Vicky. "What Does Your Dad Do for a Living? Children of Prisoners and Their Experiences of Stigma." *Children and Youth Services Review* 90 (2018): 21–27.

Sidanius, Jim, and Felicia Pratto. *Social Dominance: An Intergroup Theory of Social Hierarchy and Oppression.* New York: Cambridge University Press, 2001.

U.S. Congress. *House of Representatives-Thursday, March 26, 1992* Congressional Record, 1992.

———. *House of Representatives-Wednesday, April 20, 1994* Congressional Record, 1994.

———. *Senate-Wednesday, February 9, 1994* Congressional Record, 1994.

Watson, Stevie, Osei Appiah, and Corliss G Thornton. "The Effect of Name on Pre-interview Impressions and Occupational Stereotypes: The Case of Black Sales Job Applicants." *Journal of Applied Social Psychology* 41, no. 10 (2011): 2405–20.

Woodruff, Judy, and Daniel Bush. "Mcconnell: Some Republicans Think 'We Have Already Done Enough' Pandemic Aid." *Newshour*, 2020. https://www.pbs.org/newshour/show/mcconnell-some-republicans-think-we-have-already-done-enough-pandemic-aid.

Yancey, George. "Experiencing Racism: Differences in the Experiences of Whites Married to Blacks and Non-Black Racial Minorities." *Journal of Comparative Family Studies* 38, no. 2 (2007): 197–213.

5   The X on Your Back

Let me tell you about one particular incident where I went to a call center. And there was about, I don't know, maybe a couple dozen people and they had these computer terminals set up and everyone had to take this skills-aptitude type test. And when we finished, the administrator came out absolutely raving, just fawning over me, because she said that I scored the highest score of that test that they had ever seen. She's talking to me about a managerial position and a future with the company, and then she asked me to wait and she stepped away. A few minutes later she came back and her demeanor toward me changed drastically. She wasn't raving and fawning anymore. She asked me to step in another room and wait there. And then two men came, and they said the policy of that particular company was that they didn't hire convicted felons, so I wouldn't be working there. And then they escorted me off the property. No job.[1]

While the story above is a common experience for people who have been released from prisons, you might be surprised at the uncommon person who spoke it. Hassan Assad is best known to the world as World Wresting Entertainment (WWE) professional wrestler MVP, a decorated champion, legendary wrestler, and leader of "The Hurt Business," the group of wrestlers currently dominating WWE's flagship program, Monday Night RAW. I'm fortunate enough to call Assad a friend and invited him to speak at the first TEDxUAMonticello where he spoke the above words in his aptly titled TEDx Talk, "When do I stop being a criminal?" As illustrated through his talk, all former prisoners, whether celebrity or not, experience convictism.

A Sentence without a Period

As I teach my students, punctuation is incredibly important in writing. Whether it finishes with a punctuation mark, a question mark, or most

DOI: 10.4324/9781003189947-5

commonly a period, every sentence has an end before the new one begins. Every sentence but one. Like everyone else who has served time, Assad discovered that convictism does not stop when your prison sentence ends. Despite the fact that 95% of inmates will be released at some point and over half a million people leave prison walls each year, whether on parole or because they've completed their time, they still face a significant systemic bias once they have returned to the, as they are fond of calling it, freeworld.[2]

Prison is often commonly referred to as "paying your debt to society." That is, unfortunately, an extremely poor analogy. Imagine that you, like so many Americans, racked up thousands of dollars in debt in credit cards, student loans, and a mortgage. Maybe you took Dave Ramsey's advice and paid them off over a period of ten to twenty years. Once you made the last payment, you would celebrate because you had paid your debt. You would finally be free. Now imagine that the month after you paid off your loan, a debt collector calls to demand more money. You think they'd obviously made a mistake, but no. They tell you that no matter what you do, you'll be required to keep making payments for the rest of your life. That is the case with former inmates facing the brutal reality of convictism.

Criminal background checks abound everywhere. When they try to rent an apartment, background check. When they apply for a job, background check. Maybe they decide to finally go to college, since they couldn't do it behind bars after Pell grants were cancelled for them. You guessed it. Another background check. Where background checks used to be an expensive ordeal limited to large corporations and government offices, the outgrowth of technology has made this possible for businesses, landlords, and schools of practically any size. A quick Google search reveals dozens of companies offering bargain background checks with names like *CheckPeople*, *TruthFinder*, *Intelius*, and *CheckMate*. You can even run background checks on your phone with apps like *FedCheck* and *Offender Locator*. The wide availability of background checking technology in concert with state and federal laws and policies legitimizing discrimination against former prisoners means that convictism can more easily spread with seriously detrimental consequences.

No House

When a person is released from prison in Texas, they are given a set of civilian clothes, a check for $50, and a bus pass. The only other things they exit prison gates carrying are the remainder of funds on their trust accounts, if they have any, and few personal belongings they carry in red or white mesh bags. In many cases, these contain only paperwork, ramen noodles, medication, and toilet paper. Unless they had shoes of their own, they leave in their prison-issued boots whose rubber soles are engraved to mark the word "offender" with each step they take in the dirt. While other states may offer a bit more money, up to $200, others offer less, down to $25. Whatever the amount, this is barely enough for a night or two at a cheap motel. In roughly a third of states, they leave with no money at all.[3] For those who do get money, there typically awaits an army of shady characters outside the gates ready to fleece them of the little money they do have. Outside the infamous TDCJ Huntsville Unit, best known as Walls, a gas station nearby has a backwards facing billboard directed at the prison offering to cash their checks for free, only to sell them overpriced goods like prepaid phones. If they venture to the bus stop, a hoard of conmen awaits them, ready to sell them cheap goods to those former prisoners who have served decades and are unaware of the steep and unethical markup. As quick as their money is received, it is snatched up by these vultures and these former prisoners are left with nothing but second-rate goods and the clothes on their back. It is of little wonder, then, that many former prisoners spend their first night outside a prison cell sleeping on the streets.[4]

Homelessness remains a significant problem for former prisoners after release. Up to one in four former prisoners becomes homeless within their first year out of prison.[5] A significant reason for this, in addition to the lack of available employment covered later in this chapter, is that many landlords and apartment complexes are unwilling to lease homes to people with criminal convictions.[6] Even homeless shelters sometimes perform criminal background checks and deny admission to people who have been convicted of things like assault and armed robbery.[7] "While these forms of exclusion are enacted by individuals, they are also the result of policies that consider incarceration or criminal justice history as legal and valid reasons to deny housing."[8] Numerous federal and state government policies not only are convictist themselves, but embolden private citizens, businesses, and nonprofits to be as well.

Remember that former prisoners are only leaving with at most $200 in most cases. Due to this, those without support of family and friends live in extreme poverty and rely on programs like federally subsidized housing to survive.[9] Even there, in programs designed to help the poor, former inmates against face convictist discrimination as restrictions on their ability to access these programs have become more stringent in the form of 'one strike' policies, mandatory bans imposed on those evicted for drug or criminal involvement, and expanded discretion granted to local public housing authorities to evict tenants and restrict access to subsidies because of a criminal record or prior incarceration.[10]

Often, the only places they can find housing at all are in their old neighborhoods.[11] complete with the high crime rates and low employment opportunities that helped set them on their lawbreaking patterns in the first place.[12]

Achieving a stable home is perhaps the foundational factor in preventing recidivism.[13] Having a place to live can "provide access to spaces that allows formerly incarcerated people to parent their children, obtain jobs, desist from crime, avoid reincarceration due to parole violations, resist addiction or establish health promoting behaviors."[14] A lack of stability, on the other hand, is likely to leave them in survival mode. Without the first tier of Maslow's Hierarchy of Needs met, they will constantly be searching for ways to keep themselves fed and safe, which often means committing more crimes. These perhaps well-intentioned policies of landlords and housing authorities which they believe will keep their communities safe only raise the crime rate.

No Job

Much like Assad's experience, many former prisoners face convictism when they seek gainful employment. Unlike him, though, the conditions of incarceration are such that many lack necessary skills to get a job in the first place. Many jobs require a high school diploma or GED and some kind of work experience.[15] Without funding for education, prisoners who enter without a diploma often leave without one. Additionally, many prisoner jobs involve menial labor that does not provide any substantive training for the demands of the American workforce.[16] Furthermore, the sad reality is that even absent these factors, almost every job requires at bare minimum the ability to read and write, which some released prisoners lack.[17] Even those former inmates who have those skills, however, face significant barriers to employment.

At the height of the prison education movement in 1976, more than two-thirds of employers were willing to hire former prisoners.[18] Two decades later in 1996, two years after the passage of the crime bill which stripped prisoners of Pell grant eligibility, that percentage had plummeted to a mere 12%.[19] Unfortunately, even that minimal amount is too high as research has demonstrated that employers are far more willing to say they will hire former inmates than actually do it. One study that surveyed employers on their attitudes toward hiring ex-convicts and then sent them job applications that listed criminal convictions found that as little as one in 12 employers who said they were open to hiring former felons actually would.[20] Another study found that less than one in four businesses had ever hired a former prisoner of any type.[21]

Those few businesses that were willing to hire released prisoners also were not open to all who had served sentences. For instance, those convicted of substance abuse charges like drug use[22] and driving while intoxicated[23] were more welcomed by employers. On the other hand, those with violent and sexual criminal histories were far more excluded from hiring.[24] Despite this difference, it is interesting that most employer objection to hiring released inmates are due to a perceived lack of people skills and job training rather than the risk of them committing further crimes.[25] The prospective employers also feared that both coworkers and customers would be uncomfortable with former prisoners being employed by them, establishing how convictism continues to contribute to a lack of employment.

Like housing, employment is a crucial need for the formerly incarcerated. Due to the effects of systemic convictism, the "foremost challenge for [former prisoners] is finding legitimate employment which contributes to their successful reintegration as well as affects the overall prosperity of their community."[26] Without that, they have little to no means to provide for themselves and their families and often return to committing crime as a means to survive.[27] While those who leave prison with degrees find much more success at gaining employment than those who do not, the convictist bias against hiring them still remains.

No Vote

As a result of convictism, "formerly incarcerated people confront an array of criminal justice and social welfare policies that define a prison stay as an irredeemable mark, limit opportunities for rehabilitation and success, and restrict access to full citizenship."[28] When faced with such gigantic legal obstacles, other groups might launch campaigns to elect officials to overturn these unfavorable laws. However, as much as former prisoners might want to do so, in many cases they are unable because they are prohibited from voting.

The only places where a person never loses their right to vote as a result of criminal conviction are Maine, and Vermont. In those places, even current prisoners are able to cast their ballots. For the rest of the United States, criminal conviction means losing the right to vote for your time behind bars and often beyond. In 17 states and the District of Columbia, released prisoners including those on parole may vote. In three more, they can vote when off parole. In 19 states, the right to vote comes back after completing prison, parole, probation, and other conditions of release. Finally, in nine states, some or all convicted citizens either require direct government action to restore their rights or never regain the right to vote.

Alabama, Delaware, Iowa, Kentucky, Mississippi, and Tennessee permanently remove voting rights for anyone convicted of certain crimes. While the lists vary from state to state, they include violent crimes like murder, manslaughter, and assault; sex crimes like rape, sexual assault, and the distribution of child pornography; financial crimes like embezzlement and theft; crimes interfering with law enforcement like perjury and bribery; and acts supporting or committing terrorism. Intriguingly, Alabama includes sodomy, despite that law being struck down by the Supreme Court in *Lawrence v. Texas* 14 years before they added it to their list of disqualifying crimes, and Mississippi includes bigamy.

Even efforts to restore voting rights to the formerly incarcerated have been thwarted by convictism. In 2018, the people of Florida voted for a citizen-initiated constitutional amendment that would automatically restore voting rights upon completion of a sentence. In response, the conservative Republican-controlled legislature redefined completion of a sentence to include payment of all fines and court fees, despite this being against the express language of what the citizens of Florida voted for. As people continue to complain about the high percentage of Americans who do not vote in elections, it is important to remember that convictist policies are the reasons that millions of those not voting cannot vote.

Resisting Convictism[29]

Recently, I sold my home, and I've got some things up in the air, so I decided, well, I don't want to buy another house yet. I'm going to rent until I decide what I want to do and where I want to go. So I told my real estate agent "show me a few places," we looked around. I submitted a lease application with a non-refundable fee. Background check. For a crime I committed when I was 16 years old. I'm 45 now, so we're talking nearly 30 years ago. Background check. Lease application denied and my fee wasn't refunded. All right. That happens. Second lease application. Background check, denied! Third lease application, DENIED! I'm MVP, man! I'm on TV, your kids play with my action figures! I'm in video games! I've been in movies! I go to prisoners and I give talks to prisoners. I work with at-risk youth. I have done everything that I possibly can to show you that, like Canada says, I'm rehabilitated. But unfortunately, a segment of society still sees me as a potential threat. So when John or Jane Doe are being released from prison, when they get out, they're not MVP.[30]

While Assad continued to experience convictism despite his celebrity, he was eventually able to rent a home and is back to headlining WWE television. Despite Candace Owens' claims, some former inmates appear to experience less harsh effects of systemic convictism than others. For example, while Owens claimed Floyd could be neither a hero or martyr, formerly incarcerated celebrities have achieved both. As I wrote in an op-ed for the *Arkansas Democrat-Gazette* that critiqued Owens' convictist statement, Robert Downey Jr., who has previous convictions involving cocaine, heroin, and an unlicensed firearm, "can be a superhero who's the lead in three of the top 10 grossing films of all time, including the top film, *Avengers: Endgame*."[31] On the martyr side, Tim Allen, who served federal time for drug trafficking, was "held up by conservatives as a martyr for political correctness when ABC canceled his hit show *Last Man Standing*, allegedly due to his public support of Trump."[32] Celebrity former inmates like Assad, Downey Jr., and Allen do not completely escape convictism, but found huge economic success. Why is it that they are able to be successful when "John or Jane Doe" cannot? They won the neoliberal game.

Animosity Can Be Changed

A recognition of the current mediated discourses surrounding prisoners, criminals, prisons, and crime along with the methods by which the public adopts these views is critical to the creation of a mediated counter narrative. Returning to the modified version of Entman and Rojecki's spectrum, I argue that the general public falls into the Animosity category Neoliberalism itself, despite its damaging attributions, arguably places the public squarely in Animosity. To believe that there is a fundamental difference between criminals/prisoners and the general public is antithetical to the neoliberal fiction of free choice and equal playing field. For example, one could not simultaneously believe that criminals/prisoners are sentenced because of the choices they freely made and that criminals/prisoners are a distinct and lower group from the viewers. Therefore, the neoliberal masse is likely to hold animosity, rather than pure prejudice, against criminals and prisoners.

According to Entman and Rojecki, "animosity boils down to stereotyping, denial, political rejection and demonization, and fearful, angry emotions."[33] Stereotyping involves classifying all members of a group based on limited observation. Denial, in the manner Entman and Rojecki employ it, consists of rejecting the existence of "discrimination and structural impediments."[34] that may contribute to criminal behavior and instead attributing deviance to personal failure. Political rejection and demonization occur when individuals view the goals of another group as competitive, as opposed to cooperative, with their own. "Politics to them is generally a zero-sum game pitting [Criminal/ Prisoner] interests against [Non-criminal/non-prisoner]."[35] Viewing politics as a zero-sum game, however, meant that in the debates about Pell grants, any financial aid given to prisoners was being wrongfully taken away from college students. Finally, the fourth category of fearful and angry emotions happens when viewers experience anxiety over the potential harm criminals and prisoners might inflict upon them.

The source of the feelings and behaviors experienced by those in the Anxiety category is not prejudice or bigotry, but "rooted in sheer ignorance."[36] Given the limited contact most people have with the penal system, they remain largely unaware of the differing life circumstances that lead some to crime and others to college. The good news here is that because their beliefs are rooted in ignorance, rather than hatred, "they do not hold consistently to all their antagonistic sentiments. That is to say, *they are susceptible to change.*"[37]

Ignorance is solved primarily through education. However, to be effective, rhetoric that challenges this ignorance must consider the conditions of the audience. While neoliberal ideology is foundational in creating an audience that is receptive to the current negative discourses about criminals and prisoners, it is not so much the cause of the problem but a tool that can be coopted for alternative purposes. Since neoliberalism has been the dominant ideology since World War II, most of the public cannot remember a time when it was not the dominant cultural force. The myth of the American Dream itself relies on neoliberal ideas about personal choices leading to life consequences. Any attempt to detach the public from such deeply held taken-for-granted beliefs is likely to fail as viewers will wholly reject the argument and cling more tightly to their beliefs. Ava DuVernay's documentary, *The 13th*, is one such failure. The film, which largely mirrored arguments from Michelle Alexander's book, *The New Jim Crow* about racist policies which lead to an overrepresentation of Black men and women in prison, was critically well-received... but only among viewers that were already inclined to believe its arguments. The general public, who elected racist Donald Trump as President of the United States a month after the film's release, were not ready to accept DuVernay's narrative.

Weaponizing Neoliberalism against Itself

Instead of trying to dismantle neoliberalism, I propose utilizing it to counter the current mediated discourses. As an example of this, I turn to what might be an unlikely source: professional wrestling. WWE regularly produces the most-watched show on cable television, *Monday Night RAW*, which is trailed closely by its companion program *Smackdown!*. In June 2011, Phil Brooks, better known as wrestler CM Punk, launched himself into the national spotlight when he made what appeared to be a real, out-of-character, speech on *Monday Night Raw* where he critiqued the WWE for holding him back despite his work ethic. His speech received attention from major mainstream media programs including *The Jimmy Kimmel Show*, *Sports Illustrated*, and *The Jim Rome Show*, where ESPN personality Jim Rome spent an entire episode of his radio show discussing the speech. Brooks was rewarded by the viewing audience and the WWE, becoming the longest reigning WWE champion in the past several decades with a title reign lasting over a year. The speech was effective for two primary reasons: it was perceived to be real, rather than fictional, and it promoted neoliberal ideas while critiquing systems for not rewarding an individual's hard work.[38]

They key point to gain from understanding the impact of Brooks' speech is that he did not attempt to undermine the audience's belief in neoliberalism. Instead, he used that belief to his own benefit. If a neoliberal believes that a person's station in life is a result of their actions, then a system that ignores a person's hard work and punishes them due to circumstances outside their control must be offensive. By utilizing this preexisting belief, advocates against convictism can better convince the public. Rather than trying to fight neoliberalism as the cause of convictism, it can be coopted to become its undoing. For instance, advocates might utilize the concept of "debt to society" to their advantage. The public understands debt and, given its resistance to the mass forgiveness of student loans, expects them to be paid. Arguing, then, that prisoners have paid their debt to society and should not be further indebted could be a useful tool in dismantling the convictist infrastructure.

Conclusion

Throughout this process, it is crucial to remember that convictism did not spring up overnight. Greg Abbott did not wake up one morning and decide to try to kill prisoners with a pandemic. Candace Owens was not random in her proclamation that Floyd could never be a hero or a martyr. The elimination of Pell grants for prisoners was the result of decades of rhetorical maneuvering. Much like a tree that has grown to great heights over many years, convictism has deep roots that are embedded and entwined within the foundation of this country. Removing it will be no easy task, but the first step comes through recognition of it as a systemic bias.

This book will by no means solve the problem of convictism, but it is a first step. Through tracing its development through the history of the denial of Pell grants to prisoners, the past shines a line that brings the actions of today into greater clarity. Convictism is both rhetorical and material and it has significant effects on the currently and formerly incarcerated. Assad is clearly cognizant of the situation that he and other victims of convictism currently face. He closed his TEDx talk by saying:

> Even though, to some people I'm a celebrity, to some people I'm Montel Vontavious Porter, I'm MVP! To some juvenile delinquents who have come to me and said, "hey man, I saw you when you came to my detention center and, man, what you said made me change." To the convicts who have gotten out of prison who've found me and said, "dude, you inspired me so much." To them, I'm MVP. But sadly, to the people who own those homes who wouldn't rent to me, to the countries that won't allow me in, I'm not MVP. I'm still #190197. I'm an ex-convict. I'm just a convicted felon.[39]

If Assad and others are ever going to permanently be more than just convicted felons in the eyes of the American public, those fighting for the rights of prisoners and former prisoners must remain vigilant. As problematic as neoliberalism is, the American public is not going to abandon its belief in the "American Dream" anytime soon. Instead of fighting a losing war, we can use their own rhetoric against them and undermine convictism.

Notes

1 Hassan Assad, "When do I stop being a criminal? I Hassan "MVP" Assad I TEDxUAMonticello," in *TEDxUAMonticello* (YouTube, 2019), https://www.youtube.com/watch?v=bJ6-FVZ0IcY.

2 Cassandra A Atkin and Gaylene S Armstrong, "Does the concentration of parolees in a community impact employer attitudes toward the hiring of ex-offenders?" *Criminal Justice Policy Review* 24, no. 1 (2013): 71–93.

3 Jeremy Travis, *But they all come back: Facing the challenges of prisoner reentry* (The Urban Insitute, 2005).

4 Marta Nelson, Perry Deess, and Charlotte Allen, *The first month out: Post-incarceration experiences in New York City* (Oakland: University of California Press, 2011).

5 Travis, *But they all come back.*

6 Jeremy Travis and Michelle Waul, *Prisoners once removed: The impact of incarceration and reentry on children, families, and communities* (Washington, DC: Urban Insitute Press, 2003).

7 Nancy G La Vigne, Christy Visher, and Jennifer Castro, *Chicago prisoners' experiences returning home* (Washington, DC: Urban Institute Press, 2004).

8 Danya E Keene, Amy B Smoyer, and Kim M Blankenship, "Stigma, housing and identity after prison," *The Sociological Review* 66, no. 4 (2018): 800.

9 Matthew Desmond, *Evicted: Poverty and profit in the American city* (Crown, 2016).

10 Keene, Smoyer, and Blankenship, "Stigma, housing and identity after prison," 800.

11 David J Harding, Jeffrey D Morenoff, and Claire W Herbert, "Home is hard to find: Neighborhoods, institutions, and the residential trajectories of returning prisoners," *The Annals of the American Academy of Political and Social Science* 647, no. 1 (2013): 214–36.

12 Harry J Holzer, Steven Raphael, and Michael A Stoll, *Can employers play a more positive role in prisoner reentry?* (Washington, DC: Urban Institute, 2002).

13 Katharine H Bradley et al., No place like home: Housing and the ex-prisoner, 2001, Community Resources for Justice, Boston.

14 Keene, Smoyer, and Blankenship, "Stigma, housing and identity after prison," 801.

15 Harry J Holzer, *What employers want: Job prospects for less-educated workers* (New York: Russell Sage Foundation, 1996).

16 Bruce Western, *Punishment and inequality in America* (New York: Russell Sage Foundation, 2006).

17 Harry J Holzer, Steven Raphael, and Michael A Stoll, *Employment barriers facing ex-offenders*, Reentry Roundtable (Washington, DC: Urban Institute, 2003).

18 Donald Atkinson, C Abraham Fenster, and Abraham S Blumberg, "Employer attitudes toward work-release programs and the hiring of offenders," *Criminal Justice and Behavior* 3, no. 4 (1976): 335–44.

19 Shelley Albright and Furjen Denq, "Employer attitudes toward hiring ex-offenders," *The Prison Journal* 76, no. 2 (1996): 118–37.

20 Devah Pager and Lincoln Quillian, "Walking the talk? What employers say versus what they do," *American Sociological Review* 70, no. 3 (2005): 335–80.

21 Jacqueline Helfgott, "Ex-offender needs versus community opportunity in Seattle, Washington," *Federal Probation* 61 (1997): 12–24.

22 Rachelle Giguere and Lauren Dundes, "Help wanted: A survey of employer concerns about hiring ex-convicts," *Criminal justice policy review* 13, no. 4 (2002): 396–408.

23 Albright and Denq, "Employer attitudes toward hiring ex-offenders."

24 Giguere and Dundes, "Help wanted."

25 Giguere and Dundes, "Help wanted."

26 Atkin and Armstrong, "Does the concentration of parolees in a community impact employer attitudes toward the hiring of ex-offenders?" 72.

27 Alison J Shinkfield and Joseph Graffam, "Community reintegration of ex-prisoners: Type and degree of change in variables influencing successful reintegration," *International Journal of Offender Therapy and Comparative Criminology* 53, no. 1 (2009): 29–42.

28 Keene, Smoyer, and Blankenship, "Stigma, housing and identity after prison," 800.

29 This section is adapted from Adam Key, "In the first degree: A study of effective discourse in postsecondary prison education" (Ph.D. Dissertation, Texas A&M University, 2018).

30 Assad, "When do I stop being a criminal? I Hassan "MVP" Assad I TEDxUAMonticello."

31 Adam Key, "Hero or martyr," *Arkansas Democrat-Gazette* 2020, https://www.arkansasonline.com/news/2020/jun/18/hero-or-martyr/?opinion.

32 Key, "Hero or martyr."

33 Robert M Entman and Andrew Rojecki, *The black image in the white mind: Media and race in America* (New York: Wiley, 2001), 19.

34 Entman and Rojecki, *The black image in the white mind*, 19.

35 Entman and Rojecki, *The black image in the white mind*, 19.

36 Entman and Rojecki, *The black image in the white mind*, 19.

37 Entman and Rojecki, *The black image in the white mind*, 19.

38 Adam Key, ""The only thing that's real is me": CM Punk and the rhetorical framework of the American dream," *Communication Studies* 71, no. 4 (2020):601–11.

39 Assad, "When do I stop being a criminal? I Hassan "MVP" Assad I TEDxUAMonticello."

References

Albright, Shelley, and Furjen Denq. "Employer Attitudes toward Hiring Ex-Offenders." *The Prison Journal* 76, no. 2 (1996): 118–37.

Assad, Hassan. "When Do I Stop Being a Criminal? I Hassan "Mvp" Assad I Tedxuamonticello." In *TEDxUAMonticello*, YouTube, 2019. https://www.youtube.com/watch?v=bJ6-FVZ0IcY.

Atkin, Cassandra A, and Gaylene S Armstrong. "Does the Concentration of Parolees in a Community Impact Employer Attitudes toward the Hiring of Ex-Offenders?" *Criminal Justice Policy Review* 24, no. 1 (2013): 71–93.

Atkinson, Donald, C Abraham Fenster, and Abraham S Blumberg. "Employer Attitudes toward Work-Release Programs and the Hiring of Offenders." *Criminal Justice and Behavior* 3, no. 4 (1976): 335–44.

Bradley, Katharine H, RB Michael Oliver, Noel C Richardson, and Elspeth M Slayter. *No Place Like Home: Housing and the Ex-Prisoner.* Boston, MA: Crime and Justice Institute, 2001.

Desmond, Matthew. *Evicted: Poverty and Profit in the American City.* New York: Crown, 2016.

Entman, Robert M, and Andrew Rojecki. *The Black Image in the White Mind: Media and Race in America.* New York: Wiley, 2001.

Giguere, Rachelle, and Lauren Dundes. "Help Wanted: A Survey of Employer Concerns about Hiring Ex-Convicts." *Criminal justice policy review* 13, no. 4 (2002): 396–408.

Harding, David J, Jeffrey D Morenoff, and Claire W Herbert. "Home Is Hard to Find: Neighborhoods, Institutions, and the Residential Trajectories of Returning Prisoners." *The Annals of the American Academy of Political and Social Science* 647, no. 1 (2013): 214–36.

Helfgott, Jacqueline. "Ex-Offender Needs Versus Community Opportunity in Seattle, Washington." *Federal Probation* 61 (1997): 12–24.

Holzer, Harry J. *What Employers Want: Job Prospects for Less-Educated Workers.* New York: Russell Sage Foundation, 1996.

Holzer, Harry J, Steven Raphael, and Michael A Stoll. *Can Employers Play a More Positive Role in Prisoner Reentry?* Washington, DC: Urban Institute, 2002.

———. *Employment Barriers Facing Ex-Offenders.* Reentry Roundtable. Washington, DC: Urban Institute, 2003.

Keene, Danya E, Amy B Smoyer, and Kim M Blankenship. "Stigma, Housing and Identity after Prison." *The Sociological Review* 66, no. 4 (2018): 799–815.

Key, Adam. "Hero or Martyr." *Arkansas Democrat-Gazette*, 2020. https://www.arkansasonline.com/news/2020/jun/18/hero-or-martyr/?opinion.

———. "In the First Degree: A Study of Effective Discourse in Postsecondary Prison Education." Ph.D. Dissertation, Texas A&M University, 2018.

———. ""The Only Thing That's Real Is Me": Cm Punk and the Rhetorical Framework of the American Dream." *Communication Studies* 71, no. 4 (2020): 601–11.

La Vigne, Nancy G, Christy Visher, and Jennifer Castro. *Chicago Prisoners' Experiences Returning Home.* Washington, DC: Urban Institute Press, 2004.

Nelson, Marta, Perry Deess, and Charlotte Allen. *The First Month Out: Post-Incarceration Experiences in New York City.* Oakland: University of California Press, 2011.

Pager, Devah, and Lincoln Quillian. "Walking the Talk? What Employers Say Versus What They Do." *American Sociological Review* 70, no. 3 (2005): 355–80.

Shinkfield, Alison J, and Joseph Graffam. "Community Reintegration of Ex-Prisoners: Type and Degree of Change in Variables Influencing Successful Reintegration." *International Journal of Offender Therapy and comparative criminology* 53, no. 1 (2009): 29–42.

Travis, Jeremy. *But They All Come Back: Facing the Challenges of Prisoner Reentry.* Washington, DC: The Urban Institute, 2005.

Travis, Jeremy, and Michelle Waul. *Prisoners Once Removed: The Impact of Incarceration and Reentry on Children, Families, and Communities.* Washington, DC: Urban Insitute Press, 2003.

Western, Bruce. *Punishment and Inequality in America.* New York: Russell Sage Foundation, 2006.

Index

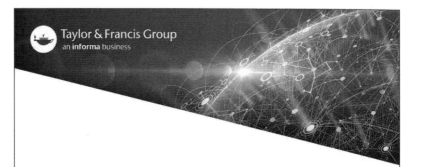

For Product Safety Concerns and Information please contact our EU
representative GPSR@taylorandfrancis.com Taylor & Francis Verlag GmbH,
Kaufingerstraße 24, 80331 München, Germany

Printed and bound by CPI Group (UK) Ltd, Croydon, CR0 4YY
11/04/2025
01844011-0003